PROTECT YOURSELF NOW!

Violence Prevention for Healthcare Workers

RAE A. STONEHOUSE

Copyright © 2020 by Rae A. Stonehouse

All rights reserved.

No part of this book may be reproduced in any form or by any electronic or mechanical means, including information storage and retrieval systems, without written permission from the author, except for the use of brief quotations in a book review.

Disclaimer: The publisher and the author are providing this book and its contents on "as is" basis and make no representations or warranties of any kind with respect to this book or its contents. The publisher and the author disclaim all such representations and warranties, including but not limited to warranties of healthcare for a particular purpose. In addition, the publisher and author assume no responsibility for errors, inaccuracies, omissions, or any other inconsistencies herein.

E-book - ISBN: 978-1-7771565-6-5
Print - ISBN: 978-1-7771565-7-2

Live For Excellence Productions
1221 Velrose Drive
Kelowna, B.C., Canada
V1X6R7
https://liveforexcellence.com

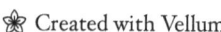 Created with Vellum

INTRODUCTION

Once upon a time it was safe to go to work. Maybe that's a fairy tale because the times have certainly changed. Increased violence has become part of our everyday life be it at home or at work. We read about it daily in the newspaper and are bombarded with violent stories from the television and radio.

As a group, healthcare workers tend to view people as being basically "good." However, reality shows us that even good people do bad things at times. Under the right circumstances [or the wrong, depending on your point of view] any of us can lose control and become aggressive. As healthcare workers we have tended to recognize violence as only arising from our patients.

A fellow worker, a manager, a client or their family or even a visitor can become potentially hazardous to us. The "bad guys" aren't always strangers to us. Working in the health care field, we regularly come in contact with people from all walks of life. It seems a grim irony that caregivers - people concerned with the welfare of others - should daily face the possibility of violence at the hands of the very people they are there to help. Yet, increasing evidence of the extent of the problem is emerging.

INTRODUCTION

PROtect Yourself! has evolved over the past 30 years or so by me, Rae Stonehouse while working as a Registered Nurse.

Years ago, while working in a mid-sized psychiatric hospital, by virtue of being a male nurse I was automatically a member of the "Goon Squad", a non-flattering term used to describe the emergency response team. I will readily admit that for the first couple of years working in psychiatry I was terrified of having to intervene physically. I was a talker, not a fighter! Now that I reflect on those days, I can't say I was all that comfortable handling verbal aggression directed at me either.

Fortunately for me, I had the opportunity to attend a week-long workshop entitled "Crisis Intervention" provided in-house. Throughout the course I learned many self- defense and physical restraining techniques I was able to utilize in my role as a psychiatric nurse.

The most important lesson learned was that the best *weapons* I possessed for self- defense purposes were my brain and my mouth. I left the workshop with a greater sense of self-confidence.

Over the years I have met and worked with many people who were confident in various aspects of their lives but were terrified when it came to intervening in a crisis where there was the likelihood it may turn physical. Even the *possibility* of physical aggression would trigger a fear response.

I have worked alongside colleagues who would "conveniently" lock themselves in the bathroom at the first sign of a potential crisis. Others have had an "emergency" phone call that needed their attention, away from the action.

I recall Mary, a fellow nurse, who was an avid sky diver. Skydiving would be an activity that I would only undertake if I was pushed out of the airplane against my will. When situations arose that required physical intervention with a disturbed patient, she was crippled with fear. After taking the Crisis Intervention program and with further on the job practice to hone her skills, Mary was able to overcome her fears of physically intervening and became an effective responder in a crisis.

INTRODUCTION

PROtect Yourself! has been developed for all the Marys out there. And the Raes too for that matter.

PROtect Yourself! provides an integrative, non-violent approach to dealing with physical aggression and verbal threat. Its method of information delivery is intended to help you develop greater awareness and vigilance, hone observational and judgment skills and to learn communication techniques to defuse potentially volatile situations. Physical interventions such as restraining techniques and break-away techniques may be mentioned throughout this manual but will not be expanded upon as they are beyond the scope of this manual.

The term "healthcare workers", encompasses a large group of people, from nurses and nursing support staff to social workers, office staff, laundry, dietary and housekeeping. If you work with people, then **PROtect Yourself!** is for you.

PROtect Yourself! is a practical "how to" manual that will enable you to...

- assess and identify disturbed/aggressive behavior
- provide effective therapeutic interventions for the benefit of your clients
- develop winning attitudes to prevent aggressive behavior
- utilize communication & leadership techniques to avoid client escalation and prevent disturbed behavior
- recognize the effects of your body language in resolving a crisis
- identify the influence that health care staff have on violence by a client
- take a proactive approach in developing worksite violence prevention protocols
- recognize a bully at work and develop strategies to minimize their damage
- recognize and support a colleague that is experiencing the effects of a critical incident

INTRODUCTION

William Feather (1889 - 1981) is often quoted as saying "knowledge is power." Mr. Feather is only partially correct. *Knowledge* is only *power* when it is *used* to achieve a goal. This program takes a *proactive* approach to minimizing the effects of violence towards those working in healthcare.

If the term *proactive* is a new concept to you, it might be helpful to see where the word is derived.

Definitions:

Activism - the policy or practice of doing things with decision and energy and emphasizing activity.

Advocacy - from the Latin ***advocare***, to summon for counsel 1) one who supports or defends a course 2) one who pleads in another's behalf.

Proactive - active in advance; anticipating trends and working to promote their development.

PROtect Yourself! follows the basic structure identified in personal protection literature i.e. the Three A's (*Awareness, Assessment, Action.*)

We will be using the following icons as road maps to keep us focused on our journey together.

INTRODUCTION

ASSESSMENT

AWARENESS

Action

We begin with an overview of violent and aggressive behavior within the healthcare field. We then explore methods and criteria for

INTRODUCTION

assessing the potential of violence. It progresses into **Crisis! What Crisis?** an exploration of the nature of crisis and systematically develops strategies to effectively diffuse a crisis.

We discuss a recently recognized form of workplace violence, that of bullying and horizontal/vertical violence. This develops into an exploration of two possible consequences of workplace violence: Post Traumatic Stress Disorder (PTSD) and "burnout".

Finally, therapeutic communication skills are explored, and we look at proactive techniques and resources you can utilize in developing a violence prevention program for your own worksite.

Throughout this manual I have used what I refer to as the "onion" method of instruction. That is, we look at a particular point, explore it, then peel back another layer and study it once again, perhaps from a different angle. It is important to note that many of us likely believe that violent behavior comes without warning and from the least expected source. This isn't always true. The warning signs are there if we are tuned to them.

We need to be *vigilant* and *proactive* in our goal to prevent workplace violence. This is a practical manual in dealing with workplace violence. You will find extensive use of bulleted lists and checklists. Some of these lists are called "Quick Lists." This has been done intentionally so you can take them and use them as a tool in your work-site. Start talking about violence in your workplace. The silence has gone on for far too long!

Author's Note * This manual has developed from many years of personal experience by the author. Much of the information has been gleaned from other sources and repackaged into a form that is practical, yet easy to use.

Whilst every effort has been taken to ensure accuracy in the preparation of the material in this manual, the author shall neither have liability nor responsibility to any person or entity with respect to any loss or damage caused or alleged to be caused directly or indirectly by the information contained within.

INTRODUCTION

The purpose of this manual is to educate and suggest strategies to reduce the likelihood you will be injured at work. It does not constitute a definitive or authoritative statement of the law.

SECTION ONE:
THE PROBLEM OF VIOLENCE IN THE WORKPLACE

CHAPTER 1
OVERVIEW: THE PROBLEM OF VIOLENCE IN THE WORKPLACE

Awareness

There is a disturbing trend in our society towards violence and it is clearly reflected in the growing number of incidents of physical, verbal, and emotional acts of violent, aggressive, assaultive and/or threatening behavior being reported to police.

A report by the Ministry for Women's Equality [British Columbia, Canada (1999)] noted that one in four women is the victim of domestic violence. Sadly, this trend is reflected in the growing violence against health care providers, most of which are women.

In community care settings, incidents are also on the rise as community care providers care for more high-risk clients. Incidents involving aggressive language, slapping, biting, and kicking, while less frequently reported, are also part of the violence toward health care providers.

Statistics would seem to indicate that violence within healthcare is on the rise. I was taught to be wary of statistics. There is an old adage "Figures never lie, but liars can figure." Now, I'm not saying that statisticians are liars, but statistics can be used to illustrate any point. The biggest criticism against current workplace violence statistics is they do not reflect the true picture.

One reason cited is that violence in the workplace will not always be reported to the employer. The worker may see the event as trivial or accept some amount or degree of violence as part of the job description. Alternatively, the worker may perceive there will be no benefit or value in reporting the incident to the employer. Some may feel they might be blamed for the incident and their job may be placed at risk if they report it.

Violence at work may also *not* be reported to the police. Again, the incident may be seen as trivial and as part of the job. Or it may be that the perpetrator of the violence would not likely be charged criminally, given his or her state of mind. This is particularly true of violence from elderly, psychiatric or mentally handicapped clients.

In 1986, while I was working in a psychiatric hospital, a patient purposely attacked and assaulted me. I contacted our local police department and tried to press charges. They just laughed at me and told me that it was part of my job just as it was part of theirs. They said they would press charges if I really wanted to but "why bother the guy was crazy, anyway." I'll leave you to your own thoughts on that one.

Finally, workers are often reluctant to report violence to their Worker's Compensation Board. Again, the incident may be viewed as trivial, or as part of the job risk. As mentioned before, how many workers are cautious of reporting because of the idea that they may lose their jobs? It seems to be the new reality that there are people lining up at the door for our job if we can't do it [or some employers would have us believe!] In addition, many workers may see the claims process, i.e. completing the WCB [Workers Compensation] forms, as being too cumbersome. They might bypass this requirement by phoning in sick, utilizing their short-term sick leave. You have to wonder how many employers encourage the worker to "book off sick" rather than make a WCB claim. This would keep the employer's assessment premiums lower. Some workers may erroneously believe that by completing a claims form they are admitting they were at fault or blame be placed on them for the incident.

The intent of this manual is to focus on violence in the workplace, specifically in a healthcare setting. Recent statistics consistently relate that the nursing profession is composed of 98% women. It is difficult to separate the concept of "work" and "nonwork." A British Columbia, Canada, initiative "***Live Violence Free***" from 1998 stated the following facts about Violence Against Women:

Because such a small percentage of violent crime is reported, especially spousal and sexual assaults where women are the primary victims, many of the statistics used in the Live Violence Free information sheets were taken from the Violence Against Women Survey. This 1993 survey by Statistics Canada is the only statistically reliable report on women's experience of violence.

The survey found that:

- 5.38 million Canadian women have experienced violence (of 10.5 m over 18 yrs.)
- One in four Canadian women were victims of assault by a spouse or partner.
- One in three Canadian women were victims of sexual assault.
- Women are the victims in four out of five spousal murders according to 1997 homicide statistics.
- One in two B.C. women were victims of sexual assault.

- One in three B.C. women were victims of assault by a spouse or partner.
- One in six B.C. women were victims of sexual attack by a date or boyfriend.

Young women's experience of violence

The 1993 Adolescent Health Survey in British Columbia found that:

- 32% of girls and 15% of boys between grades 7 - 12 had been sexually and/or physically abused.

Grade 11 girls experienced the highest rate of abuse:

—28% had been physically abused;

—28% had been sexually abused.

The previous statistics are Canadian and may be considered dated, but should serve to illustrate the connection between violence at home i.e. nonwork activities and the workplace.

Let's look at the concept of ***violence*** a little closer.

CHAPTER 2
THE MOST RECOGNIZABLE FORMS OF VIOLENCE:

The Most Recognizable Forms of Violence Include:

Physical Assault such as punching, hitting, kicking, slapping, shoving, biting, choking, using a weapon, withholding medicines or medical treatment, or threatening to do any of the above.

SEXUAL ASSAULT SUCH AS FORCING ANY KIND OF SEXUAL ACTIVITY on someone without that person's consent, even in a marriage.

Violence also includes:

- **Emotional abuse** such as: making a person feel worthless; telling them they are the problem; that they invite violence or they need psychological help; humiliating them in front of others; not allowing them to visit friends or family; showing extreme jealousy; withholding documents like immigration or refugee papers; threatening deportation, or depriving someone of their freedom whether in their public or private life.

- **Verbal Abuse** such as: telling a person they're stupid; yelling, screaming, name-calling, or using sarcasm and put-downs; threatening to hurt a person.

- **Sexual Harassment** such as: unwanted and suggestive comments or actions of a sexual nature; slurs, jokes, gestures regarding sexuality; unwanted physical contact; requests for sexual favors; or comments about an individual's sexual orientation or identity.

- **Economic abuse** such as: controlling money or stopping a person from getting a job or education.

CHAPTER 3
THE IMPACT OF WORKPLACE VIOLENCE ON WORKERS

Workplace violence may result in physical and/or psychological injuries to the worker as follows:

Workers

Physical injury/Psychological injury:

- Grief, denial, self-blame
- Depression, anger, disbelief
- Anxiety, shock, apathy
- Dependency, helplessness
- Symptoms of PTSD (post-traumatic stress disorder)
- Fear of future threats or injury
- Self-doubt
- Powerlessness
- Fear of returning to work
- Decreased job performance
- Changes in relationships with co-workers/families
- Extended time off
- Physical illness
- Sleep pattern disturbances

- Headaches
- Impaired stress management and substance abuse

Co-workers

Psychological impact:

- Denial, self-blame
- Blaming of victim, leading to conflict or distrust among co-workers
- Anger, increased stress
- Fear for their own safety
- Lower workplace morale
- Re-distribution of the workload due to the worker's leave as a result of physical and/or psychological injury

Editorial Comment: You may notice that many of the statistics quoted throughout this manual are related to nursing in British Columbia, Canada. From a purely statistical standpoint they can easily be dismissed as being too small of a number to generalize as to the incidence of violence in a worldwide nursing profession. It is not the intent of this book to provide up-to-date statistics that are applicable to the reader's geographical region. If these statistics are important to you I suggest that you research your respective Occupational Health & Safety organizations and Workers Compensation Boards.

Having said that, the intent of this manual is to serve as a resource to you in providing practical techniques in dealing with workplace violence.

CHAPTER 4
ASSAULT/ABUSE DIRECTED TOWARDS CARE-GIVER

An Overview

- Assaults include both physical and verbal aggression.
- Assaults include: punching, kicking, throwing objects, spitting, biting and severe verbal abuse.
- Assaults may be either unprovoked as staff perform their duties or sustained as a direct result of staff interventions.

THE SEVERITY OF INJURIES VARIES GREATLY. THREE DEGREES OF injury have been identified: (*physical contact must have taken place*)

- **First degree:** no physical injury detectable.
- **Second degree:** includes minor injuries such as bruises, abrasions and small lacerations.
- **Third degree:** large lacerations, fractures and loss of consciousness, as well as injuries resulting in permanent physical disability or death.

Let's look at the concept of assault a little closer and try to define it.

- **Assaults include both physical and verbal aggression.**

Proactive Tip: We tend to think of assault in just physical terms, someone hurting us, but yelling, swearing, threatening, name calling can be just as devastating, especially if the person is capable of following through on the threats. Later we explore the act of "horizontal violence" which includes the afore mentioned actions but from a surprising source.

- **Assaults include: punching, kicking, throwing objects, spitting, biting and severe verbal abuse.**

Editorial Comment: Throughout my career I've been involved in situations where I have been punched, kicked and almost had my thumb bitten off. I have had ashtrays; books; glasses; chairs; coffee; and pop thrown at me. I've been spit at, and on and called every profanity that I was aware of and some that I wasn't.

- **Assaults may be either unprovoked as staff perform their duties or sustained as direct result of staff interventions.**

Editorial Comment: I've known fellow workers who have been hit with canes and walkers. While I was working with mentally challenged adults with major psychosis, one of my fellow female coworkers experienced a patient attempting to use her head as a battering ram, trying to knock the bricks out of a concrete wall. While working on a psychogeriatric ward I reached under one elderly fellow's sheets to see if he was dry and got a "knuckle sandwich" in the face for my efforts.

Let's look at *injuries* resulting from these assaults.

The severity of injuries varies greatly. Three degrees of injury have been identified: (physical contact must have taken place)

- **First degree: no physical injury detectable.**

You might have been pushed or shoved, maybe shaken up, but with no visible injury resulting.

- **Second degree: includes minor injuries such as bruises, abrasions and small lacerations.**
- **Third degree: large lacerations, fractures and loss of consciousness, as well as injuries resulting in permanent physical disability or death.**

PROACTIVE TIP: ONE STUDY INDICATED THAT AFTER BEING assaulted some staff members reported experiencing fright, anger, and apprehension. Sleep disturbances, intrusive memories, and hyper vigilance were also reported. The example I gave earlier of the young woman who was used as a battering ram would certainly be an example of this. She had headaches and nightmares for a year or so after the incident.

THESE SYMPTOMS HAVE BEEN IDENTIFIED AS BEING ASSOCIATED WITH Post Traumatic Stress Symptoms (PTSD). PTSD is discussed later in this book.

CHAPTER 5
DEFINITIONS OF VIOLENT & AGGRESSIVE BEHAVIOR

Before we look at the definitions, it might be helpful to draw from the area of interpersonal communication known as *"assertiveness."*

BEHAVIORALLY, AN INDIVIDUAL WHO IS ASSERTIVE CAN ESTABLISH close, interpersonal relationships; can protect themselves from being taken advantage of by others; can make decisions and free choices in life; can recognize and acquire more of his/her interpersonal needs; and can verbally and non-verbally express a wide range of feelings and thoughts, (both positive and negative).

THIS IS TO BE ACCOMPLISHED WITHOUT EXPERIENCING UNDUE amounts of anxiety or guilt and without violating the rights and dignity of others in the process.

ABUSE, ASSAULT AND VIOLENCE ARE TERMS USED INTERCHANGEABLY in the literature to describe behaviors ranging from verbal abuse and emotional harm, to criminal activities such as common assault (which includes wounding, maiming, disfiguring, or endangering life).

WE CAN CONSIDER THREE TERMS IN HELPING TO DEFINE THE AREA of aggression and violence.

THESE ARE:

- Assertion
- Aggression
- Violence

1. ***Assertion*** is a generic term for all behavior, as described above, without hostile intent, which is designed to gratify a need.

(Assertion (Latin asserera; claim, affirm) To state positively, to affirm, to maintain insistently)

1. ***Aggression*** is a specific form of assertion that has hostile intent.

(Aggression (Latin aggressio; a going towards, attack)

VIOLENCE PERTAINS TO THE USE OF PHYSICAL FORCE AND IS THE exertion of physical force to injure or abuse.

(Violence (Latin violentia; vehemence, ferocity)

The use of definitions vary between organizations, therefore the following definitions will be used to define the behavior that this manual is targeting.

(a) Workplace Violence is:

- a hostile or aggressive behavior resulting in physical or emotional injury to [Hospital] staff members or damage to [Hospital] property. The incident or act may be committed by a patient, resident, volunteer, visitor, physician or staff member and may involve but is not limited to name calling, swearing, threats, use of a weapon, sexual harassment, assault and/or battery, any of which may occur in the normal course of the regular duties and job responsibilities.

(b) Assault is:

any action by another which creates a situation in which a person has reasonable cause to feel afraid for his or her safety, whether or not an injury (physical or psychological) occurs.

Comment: The two components of assault are the ***threat*** and the ***ability*** of the person to carry out the threat. Examples of assault are hits, grabs, shoves, kicks, pinches, sexual assaults, threats with an object such as a chair, cane or sharps container, or with a dangerous weapon such as a knife, gun or blunt instrument, any physical injury, and verbal hostility and abuse.

(c) Aggression is:

- the verbal or physical acting out of anger or hostile feelings. Aggressive behavior may be directed towards self, other people or objects and may include everything from: agitation, restlessness, threatened aggression, offensive gestures to destruction of environment, self-abuse and physical injury to others.

Threats:

- Threats generally involve any communication of intent to injure that gives a worker reasonable cause to believe there is a risk of injury. A threat against a worker's family arising from the worker's employment is considered a threat against the worker.

Examples of threats include:

- Threats (direct or indirect) delivered in person or through letters, phone calls, or electronic mail
- Intimidating or frightening gestures such as shaking fists at another person, pounding a desk or counter, punching a wall, angrily jumping up and down and screaming
- Throwing and striking objects
- Stalking
- Wielding a weapon, or carrying a concealed weapon for the purpose of threatening or injuring a person

Editorial Comment: Years ago, while working in a psychiatric hospital, I received a phone call from a distraught family member of a patient who was incarcerated under a Warrant of the Lieutenant Governor, having committed murder. I was told "I know where you live and I'm coming to get you and your family."

As one might expect, this was quite disturbing. I first notified my wife and advised her of the situation. I then notified my shift supervisor who was of little help. "I don't know… do whatever you think needs to be done Rae…"

I notified the police and they apprehended the individual. Alcohol was a factor in the individual making the call and they were not considered being an ongoing threat. The situation was rather unsettling and has definitely been influential in my promoting workplace violence prevention.

CHAPTER 6
SIGNS OF DISTURBED BEHAVOUR

Q uick List

It is important to be aware of *"**signs**"* that may indicate impending violence, aggression or assault. Be alert for the following warning signs:

PACING

Hyperactivity

Muttering

Swearing, chanting, loud speech or shouting

Exaggerated movements

Sudden movements or pointing

Staring

Avoiding Eye Contact

Eyes Narrowed

Looking angry, threatening stance

Body tensed (neck, jaw, arms)

Rapid respirations and flared nostrils

Clenched fists

Restlessness

Withdrawal

Rocking

Banging Objects

Restlessness

Threatened Aggression

Destruction of Physical Property

Self-Abuse

Physical Aggression

Signs & Symptoms of Aggressive Behavior

Disturbed behavior can easily escalate into aggressive behavior. It is important to be aware of the early warning signals, such as restlessness, toe tapping, pacing, and the expression of fear, anxiety, anger, frustration, loss, hopelessness, despair.

These emotions communicate the potential for aggressive behavior toward others, self or property.

Proactive Tip:

* Acknowledge these feelings with the person. This is the single most effective form of defusing and preventing aggression at the early stages.

Emotional Clues

We can gain valuable information from their conversation or observing their outward emotional state.

Examples of emotional clues you can expect to encounter are as follows:

Disorientation:

Comments/Questions?

"Where am I?"

"What's going on?"

"Where's my wife/husband?"

"Who are you?"

"Why am I here?"

Observable Behavior: acting restless, they look like they don't belong where they are

Fear:

Comments/Questions?

"Am I going to be all right?"

"Is everything OK?"

"I'm afraid!"

OR THE *OPPOSITE* WHERE THEY APPEAR READY TO DEFEND themselves i.e. hyper alert asking (aggressive) demanding questions...

"WHAT'S GOING ON?"

"What are you doing about...?"

"What are you doing to me?"

FRUSTRATION:

Comments/Questions?

"Why me?"

"How can this be happening to me?"

OBSERVABLE BEHAVIOR: THEY MAY BE SHORT-TEMPERED, CRANKY, argumentative, bothered by what may be considered trivial matters and have audible sighs.

FEELINGS OF INADEQUACY:

Comments/Questions:

"It'll never work!"

"Why me?"

"I am a loser."

"I'm too stupid."

"I can never do that."

"Nobody likes me."

"Nobody cares."

REJECTIONS (REAL OR PERCEIVED):

Comments/Questions:

"Why bother, no one cares."

"Nobody could ever love me."

"I tried that once and failed."

"I will always fail."

"They think I am a fool."

LOSS/GRIEF: (REAL OR PERCEIVED) (COULD BE LOSS OF A LOVED ONE, a friend, money, or even their reputation)

Comments/Questions:

"How could he/she do this to me?"

"What am I going to do without them?"

"I can't go on by myself"

"There is no use in living anymore."

"Nothing matters anymore."

ANGER: (COULD BE DIRECTED OUTWARDS TO OTHERS OR INWARDS TO self)

Comments/Questions:

"How dare they do that to me!"

"Who do they think they are!"

"They don't know who they're dealing with!"

"I'll show them a thing or two!"

"I guess they must be right, I am useless"

"They'll be sorry when I'm gone."

"I might as well be dead, no one cares anyway."

Behavioral Clues

Testing limits:

Comments/Questions?

"What would you do if I punched you in the stomach?"

"What would happen if I took all my pills at one time?"

"I am leaving here and there's not a thing that you can do about it!"

"How many aspirin does it take to kill a person?"

Intolerance of authority: (QUESTIONING AUTHORITY, DEFYING the rules)

Observable Behavior: frequent questions, attempts at dominating conversation or monopolizing authority figure's attention, irritability, obvious "put-downs", gossiping

Comments/Questions:

"Who died and made you God?"

"When did you go to school, if you did?"

"Who said that you're the boss?"

"We'll see about that!"

. . .

Need for personal space:

Observable Behavior: sometimes they need to pace indoors or maybe get outside, can't stand to have anyone near them

Comments/Questions:

"I need some room to breathe."

"I've got to get out of here!"

"The walls are closing in on me."

Posture:

Observable Behavior: sitting on or moving to the edge of the chair

Speech:

- rapid, high pitched

- anxious tone

- sudden voice change

- muttering

- swearing

- sighing audibly

Motor Activity:

Observable Behavior:

- unable to sit still

- appears to be tense

- pacing

- startles easily

- increased agitation

- exaggerated movements

- moving things without purpose

- darting eyes

- staring/avoiding eye contact

- retreats when approached

- not sleeping, (when they should be)

- rocking

- banging objects

- restlessness

- destruction of physical property

- tapping of hands, fingers, feet

OTHERS:

Observable Behavior:

- increased confusion

- eyes narrowed

- looking angry

- body tensed (neck, jaw, arms)

- fist clenched

- withdrawal

- threatened aggression

- self-abuse

- physical aggression

- sensitivity to noise

- refusal to take medication

- flat, dull affect

- dilated pupils, (indicator of fear)

~

CHAPTER 7
SECTION ONE SUMMARY

Violence is increasing in society and this is reflected in healthcare, a field predominantly composed of women. The statistics of workplace violence may actually be higher than reported as many incidents of violence are not reported to the employer.

We defined and described the most recognizable forms of violence as physical assault and sexual assault. We then expanded upon that definition to include: emotional abuse, verbal abuse, sexual harassment and economic abuse.

We explored how workers are impacted by violence in the workplace. We then focused on how violence presents itself in our healthcare work settings. Defining violent and aggressive behavior helped us to better understand the range of language often used in literature to describe workplace violence.

The **Signs of Disturbed Behavior Quick List** introduced us to the broad range of behaviors that we might see in our workplaces. Quick Lists are designed to be printed and discussed. Perhaps a staff meeting or in-service would be a perfect place to get the dialogue on acknowledging that workplace violence exists and to take steps toward preventing it from happening in your worksite.

We then explored the different emotions that disturbed individuals might display.

IN **SECTION TWO** WE EXPLORE RISK ASSESSMENT FOR VIOLENCE IN our work settings and triggers for aggression. We will be challenged to consider how we personally view working with potentially violent individuals and techniques to communicate with disturbed individuals are introduced.

SECTION TWO:
ASSESSMENT

CHAPTER 8
RISK ASSESSMENT FOR VIOLENCE

Purpose:

The concept of *"risk"* is fundamental to prevention and management of violence. Definitions for terms such as *"safe"*, *"unsafe"*, *"acceptable risk"*, *"unacceptable risk"* and *"high risk"* will vary according to the organization. An awareness of risk of aggression from clients due to past history of violence, life problems, anger, frustration, grief, loss or loneliness is essential-- all are contributors to the risk of aggressive behavior. Risk is also related to the environment. When the care-giver is aware of risk and has the skills to notice early warning signs of aggression, he or she will be in a better position to prevent escalation and less likely to unwittingly escalate the behavior.

Successful prevention depends on early recognition of the signs of risk and understanding of the appropriate response that will help or reduce the risk of aggressive behavior. There is a combination of factors which can be used to predict in which situation a client is more likely to be at "risk" for assaultive episodes.

RISK FACTORS FOR VIOLENCE INCLUDE:

- History of violence or assault
- Previous exposure to past incidents of aggression and violence
- Age (younger, majority age 20-40)
- Gender (males more than females)
- Alcohol/drugs (dependence/intoxication/withdrawal)
- Socio-economic status (low more than high)
- Estimated IQ (low more than high)
- Residential mobility
- Marital status (lack of)
- Violent/abusive family or friends
- Difficulty communicating
- Diagnosis (mental or physical illness or injury)
- Treatment setting
- Legal status (involuntary or voluntary)

- The environment. (crowding)
- Sensitivity to disruptive events
- Patients who feel loss of power or control
- Employee related: negative staff attitudes, new inexperienced staff with minimal education, male staff more likely to be assaulted than female, lack of or limited violence prevention training.

ANOTHER CONTRIBUTING FACTOR IS THE *APPROACH* OF THE CARE provider.

CHAPTER 9
HISTORY OF VIOLENCE

Many of those clients who lose control may never do so again; however, a past history of violence or aggressive behavior is the single most reliable predictor of future episodes. Information about a client's past history is vital in determining risk and should be communicated to the care providers in contact with that client.

The more you know about your client or resident, the more you will be able to anticipate risk. All care providers require knowledge of the client history in order to be able to assess risk.

When taking a nursing history, it is important to gather information related to past incidents of violent behavior.

Asking questions in a nonjudgmental, caring manner is very important and will help you to determine and assess risk of violence or aggression.

Many care facilities include a precaution page as part of their clinical record. History of violence, the form of violence (verbal, physical), who it was directed at, involvement with law enforcement agencies, and suicidal ideation and/or gestures should all be noted on the precaution sheet.

Criteria: Prior history of assaultive behavior

Behavior:

- has assaulted in the past
- has been violent under stress in the past
- has never been assaultive in the past

Comment: One who has been violent in the past is likely to do so again. One who has never been violent and suddenly becomes so may be suffering from organic illness.

* See Cognitive Impairment

Assessment Questions:

- How do you behave when you are anxious?
- How do you deal with your frustration?
- When people disturb or upset you how might you respond?
- What will you do when you become agitated? angry?
- How can we best help you when you become agitated or angry?
- Have you ever considered suicide?
- If so, did you have a plan?
- Did you ever make an attempt at suicide?
- Are you currently or have you ever been in trouble with the law?

* It might be necessary to ask a family member these questions!

. . .

CRITERIA: PREVIOUS EXPOSURE TO PAST INCIDENTS OF aggression and violence:

Comment: Recollection of specific stressful events that occurred in the past may cause clients to strike out at workers.

Criteria: Violent/abusive family or friends:

COMMENT: WORKERS MUST DEAL NOT ONLY WITH PATIENTS BUT also their family members and friends, sometimes in stressful circumstances. Families and friends share patient's sadness and frustration over illness and physical disability, a sense of inadequacy, and loss of control and independence. Such unhappy circumstances can turn routine contacts with workers into confrontations.

CRITERIA: DIFFICULTY IN COMMUNICATING:

Comment: Misunderstandings due to language or a lack of understanding of cultural traditions may lead to conflict between client and worker.

CHAPTER 10
DIAGNOSIS: COGNITIVE IMPAIRMENT

Reversible: Examples of causes: delirium or acute confusional state related to fluid and electrolyte imbalance; medication side effects; infection; trauma; certain types of head injuries; psychiatric disorder; substance use (alcohol, drugs); history of post-traumatic stress disorder; by anaesthetic/analgesia for pain management.

CRITERIA: INCREASE IN MOTOR AGITATION
Behavior:

- pacing
- inability to sit still
- sudden cessation of motor activity

COMMENT: THESE ARE ATTEMPTS TO DISCHARGE AGGRESSION VIA large muscle activity. This can easily escalate into acting out behavior.

. . .

CRITERIA: THREATENING VERBALIZATIONS OR GESTURES toward real or imagined objects

BEHAVIOR:

- retaliation toward actual persons who are seen as threats
- aggressiveness in response to threatening visual or auditory hallucinations
- aggressiveness in response to expansion of delusional thinking

DEMENTIA CAUSES A DECLINE IN ALL AREAS OF MENTAL ABILITY, including a person's understanding of is going on around them

COMMENT: SUCH HALLUCINATIONS ARE BIZARRE, THREATENING, unfamiliar, or confusing. Many psychotic individuals do live comfortably with an entourage of familiar "voices."

The degree of violence is related to how desperately client perceives the need to protect the self. Because there may be no obvious connection between the cause of the patient's anger and the resulting violent incident, workers may see the patient's behavior as completely unprovoked.

CRITERIA: INTENSIFICATION OF AFFECT

Behavior:

- very tense expression
- jumpiness
- elated expression

Comment: Such intensification indicates loss of control, especially if accompanied by laughing.

CHAPTER 11
CRITERIA: ALCOHOL & DRUG ABUSE AND WITHDRAWAL

Behavior:
- intoxication with drugs or alcohol
- withdrawal from drugs or alcohol

COMMENT: THE NEED TO PROVIDE CARE TO SUBSTANCE ABUSERS, and the widespread awareness that medications such as opiates are available in health care facilities contribute to violence.

CHEMICALLY DEPENDENT CLIENTS PRESENT RISK WHILE INTOXICATED or in withdrawal stages. The transition period is of high risk for violence. The client can act out rage with their inhibitions dissolved from either intoxication or withdrawal from drugs and/or alcohol. Violence is due to irritability of the central nervous system. There can be neurological damage to the cerebral cortex. The anxiety, suspicion, and sense of helplessness that comes with being in a hospital or treatment center, as well as the distress caused by the detoxification or treatment itself, can cause clients to become aggressive towards workers.

Withdrawal will be difficult to detect if you are unaware that the client has a chemical dependency problem. Some research would indicate that up to 30% of admissions to acute care facilities have a chemical dependency problem as a secondary diagnosis.

Additional Assessment Criteria:

In addition to formal screening devices, consider the following general indicators which may point to a dependency problem:

- Smell of alcohol on breath or person
- Flushed face, blood-shot eyes, bulbous nose, or facial telangiectasia (small red spider veins radiating about a center core)
- Dilated or constricted pupils
- General appearance: poor hygiene, disheveled
- Intoxicated visitors
- Is patient confused, restless, defensive, hypersensitive, anxious to leave hospital, impulsive or rebellious?
- Signs of depression: any past suicide attempts?
- Poor employment record
- No fixed address or frequent address changes
- Weekend partner: someone with a penchant for chemically fueled social experiences
- Check old charts/clinical records for frequent emergency visits, medications, broken bones, prior laboratory indicators

- Lifestyle habits
- Impaired charges or roadside suspensions
- Smoker
- Unhealthy looking due to lifestyles: too thin or overweight

Many healthcare facilities have integrated this questionnaire into the nursing assessment forms.

CAGE has proven to be a reliable tool for preliminary assessment.

C Do you ever feel you ought to **CUT** down on your drinking?

A Do you ever feel **ANGRY** or **ANNOYED** if somebody comments or questions you about your drinking?

G Do you ever feel **GUILTY** about your use of alcohol, or how you behaved under the influence?

E EYE-OPENER- Do you take a drug or drink first thing in the morning to steady nerves or get rid of a hangover?

One affirmative response indicates that further assessment is required.

With *two* positives, an 80% likelihood of dependency exists and with *three* positives, there is a 99% chance the patient is chemically dependent.

Withdrawal Assessment:

Stages of alcohol withdrawal are characterized by the following symptoms:

1) Earliest or Mild Withdrawal: sensation of uneasiness, consciousness of visceralfunction, nausea, churning, tightness, anxiety, and insomnia.

2) Minimal: fidgeting, agitation, chain smoking, drinking many cups of coffee.

3) Moderate: severe agitation, difficult to keep patient in bed, attention lapses, involuntary tremors, diaphoresis [increased sweating], tachycardia [increased heart rate], elevated blood pressure, nausea, vomiting, malaise.

4) Severe: auditory/visual hallucinations, delirium tremens (DT's), irrational fears, sensitive to noise, extreme agitation, difficult cooperating, muscular hyperactivity, severe diaphoresis.

5) Extreme: all of stage 4 symptoms, totally irrational, extreme diaphoresis and tachycardia, convulsions

Changes in Medications: Changes in or combinations of, medications require constant assessment of client behavior and condition. The distress of substituting one medication for another and the required time intervals between medications can frustrate clients and cause them to act out.

. . .

IRREVERSIBLE: DEMENTIA RELATED TO LONG STANDING ALCOHOL use, Alzheimer's disease

CHAPTER 12
CRITERIA: MEDICATIONS (PRESCRIPTION & OVER-THE-COUNTER)

Effects of Medications: Certain medications can alter a client's perception, medical condition, and actions. Because medications have different and sometimes unexpected effects on individuals, they may cause clients to become aggressive or violent towards workers. Medications such as the benzodiazepines, can have a disinhibiting effect that can result in uncharacteristically violent behavior.

Changes in Medications: Changes in or combinations of medications require constant assessment of client behaviour and condition. The distress of substituting one medication for another and the required time intervals between medications can frustrate clients and cause them to act out.

Irreversible: Dementia related to long standing alcohol use, Alzheimer's disease.

When assessing elderly clients with difficult behavior, the fundamental question to ask of the behavior is "why?" Psychiatric and physical illness will produce physical and behavioral symptoms.

Learning to ask "why?" may give the care-giver answers to questions about the elderly client's aggressive behavior leading to treatment of the conditions triggering the difficult behavior.

CRITERIA: PRESENCE OF ACUTE ORGANIC BRAIN SYNDROME

BEHAVIOR:

- sudden rise or fall in level of consciousness
- disorientation as to time, place, person
- impairment of recent memory
- auditory hallucinations within the psychic horizon (i.e. within earshot)
- visual hallucinations

COMMENT:

Sense of time is lost first. Hallucinations indicate functional mental disorder.

MENTALLY ILL CLIENTS

Statistically, it has been proven that the mentally ill are no more violent than the general population. With the implementation of the Mental Health Initiative (deinstitutionalizing of mentally ill people), the community is encountering mentally ill individuals who were previously cared for in institutions. Without adequate resources such as supportive housing, community drop-in centers, and outreach workers, mentally ill individuals tend to become more visible. They are often thrust into crisis because their basic needs are not being met.

. . .

Criteria: Acute Anxiety (panic disorders)

Assess for:

- nonverbal behavior, examples: pacing, wringing hands, picking at something, darting eyes, quick erratic movements, or withdrawal
- verbal behavior, examples: talking loudly, quickly or in a demanding voice
- a change in usual behavior

Criteria: Psychiatric Problems

Assess for:

- acute psychiatric illness
- psychotic patients with disrupted thought patterns, poor impulse control
- suffering from delusions and/or hallucinations
- suspiciousness (paranoid, not trusting)
- dual diagnosis (mental illness & chemical dependency)

CHAPTER 13
CRITERIA: PERSONALITY TRAITS

Assess for:

- personality disorders (paranoid, borderline, antisocial)
- acting out for attention

Comment:

Mental illness does not generally appear to be related to violence in the absence of a history of violent behavior.

"However, the belief that mental disorder bears some moderate association with violent behavior is both historically invariant and culturally universal." (Monahan 1992. (10).)

PHYSICAL DIAGNOSIS:

Criteria: Seizures or post seizure states (may cause disorientation and confusion)

Comment:

Many people come out of a seizure, angry, confused or fighting. They may not understand a command or recognize a familiar face and may uncharacteristically push someone away that they otherwise recognize.

Criteria: Metabolic abnormalities, drug toxicity, and acute neurologic impairment

Comment: All may trigger agitated or combative conduct.

Risk Factors for aggression in elderly clients:

- impaired cognition
- sensory loss
- immobility
- loss of environmental control
- limited social support

Comment:

Risk is highest during personal care: bathing, dressing, toileting, when client cannot visually recognize caregivers; and during day/night, night/day shifts.

CHAPTER 14
CRITERIA: ENVIRONMENT/MILIEU OF TREATMENT

Comment: There is some research which indicates that the dynamics of assault differ according to the setting. Assaults in a facility may have more to do with the setting than the individual characteristics of the client or the care provider. The combination of a client with a history of violence in a facility setting is the most widely recognized risk scenarios. Community care providers who must visit clients' homes are also at risk and should not enter a dangerous situation by themselves. Often it may not be the client who is considered dangerous, but the clients' surroundings. Request for accompaniment of a partner i.e. another care provider are risk reduction approaches.

ENVIRONMENTAL RISKS IN COMMUNITY CARE:

- Isolation of care providers in homes
- Poor lighting
- Limited visibility
- Drug and alcohol related environment

- Restricted exit
- Disruptive non-clients
- High crime area
- Distant parking

CHAPTER 15
CRITERIA: SENSITIVITY TO DISRUPTIVE EVENTS

Comment:
Certain events and circumstances may be particularly stressful to patients/clients and may raise their anxiety levels. Events that may lead to violence or aggression include:

- Personal care — feeding, bathing, toileting, mobilizing
- Visits involving family, friends, and the resulting fatigue
- Treatments such as dressing changes or physiotherapy that may cause pain or disrupt visits, rest, or leisure activity (for example, watching television)
- Treatment delays (real or perceived)
- Discharge time, which involves increased levels of noise and activity at a time when the patient/client may be feeling quite anxious
- Regimented wake-up calls and bedtimes, rigidly scheduled meal times, predetermined duration of meal times, a set amount of time for personal hygiene, and other routines that may become frustrating to patients/clients, particularly those requiring long-term care

- Noise, sleep disruption
- Lack of information from medical staff concerning diagnosis, care, test results, or prognosis
- Fear of going home

CHAPTER 16
CRITERIA: STAFFING/STAFF ATTITUDE

AWARENESS

Comments:

Research has shown that healthcare worker's behavior and actions towards individual clients may increase the chances of violence occurring. It has been theorized that patients who are potentially violent cause staff members, in their anxiety, to assume more authoritarian roles. This is more likely to trigger patient violence because it can increase the patient's feelings of helplessness.

Staff may develop preconceived attitudes or opinions about a client based on small pieces of information example: another staff's opinion, disagreeable diagnosis, and disagreeable acts in the client's past. This can lead to repressive or punitive treatment of the client.

Counter-transference has been identified as a possible indicator in the potential for client violence. The staff may project their own angry impulses onto the client and therefore, exaggerate that client's capacity for violence. This can lead to rejection, which can provoke more violence. The concept of the "self-fulfilling prophesy" readily comes to mind. If you expect the client to behave in a violent manner, and you alter your behavior to be in control, in all likelihood, the client will respond in kind.

Assess for:

- Excessive workloads: may contribute to care givers' fatigue and diminished ability to identify and subsequently handle potentially violent situations
- Working alone
- Frequent heavy use of medications, restrictions, seclusion and restraints — intrusive and most restrictive approaches
- Strict structure negating a positive milieu
- Expectations of violence as "part of the job" or common occurrence
- Lack of recognition of the possibility of risk, preventing care provider from identifying and intervening at the earliest stage
- Dislike of client
- Projected animosity
- Authoritarian attitude
- Overcontrolling behavior
- Lack of socializing with client (little person-to-person contact)
- Burnout

CHAPTER 17
TRIGGERS FOR AGGRESSION:

The literature suggests that just as many patients with pre-assaultive behaviors (verbal aggression, high activity level and invasion of personal space) never go on to assault staff as those that do. So what is it that drives the 50% of violent prone clients to assault staff?

It is generally felt that there is a "trigger" that sets off the physical aggression. It is important you have an awareness of potential "triggers" in your working environment.

One of the strongest triggers is activated when the client perceives that they are being treated with disrespect or unfairly. When healthcare workers are tired or overworked, they may become insensitive to their client's needs. Staff interaction with their clients can thus become argumentative, authoritarian, and in some cases threatening. To maintain our personal safety, we must be able to conduct a self-assessment and identify when we are displaying verbally aggressive behavior and are becoming part of the problem, rather than part of the solution.

. . .

TRIGGERS CAN INCLUDE:

- Intoxication
- Loss of a central love relationship
- Acute emotional crisis
- Loss of personal power
- Loss of face
- Fear
- Pain
- Physiological states e.g. hunger, thirst, lack of sleep, boredom and unstructured activity
- Staff rejections
- Rejection
- Disrespect
- Crowding
- Irritating patients and staff
- Tasks a patient may not want to perform

These personal attitudes have been effective when working with disturbed individuals:

- Alertness
- Sensitiveness
- Self-Awareness
- Confidence
- Respectfulness
- Belief in Equality
- Genuineness

CHAPTER 18
VIOLENCE IN THE WORKPLACE SELF-ASSESSMENT

Here are some self-assessment questions to help you to become more aware of your own feelings regarding violence and the violent client.

1) Do I have a constant sense of fear around this client?

2) Do I feel comfortable turning my back on this client?

3) Do I avoid this client?

4) Do I take sides with either the client or the family?

5) Do I feel capable of handling violent, assaultive behavior if it occurs?

6) Do I feel judgmental about the client's behavior?

7) Do I want to punish the client because of their behavior?

8) Have I become so uptight and anxious about the client that I am distorting his/her behavior in my mind?

9) Am I so angry with the client and with my fellow staff that we can no longer deal therapeutically with the client?

10) How am I coping with the feelings that I have about the client?

PROACTIVE TIP: IF YOU HAVE ANSWERED "YES" TO ANY OF THESE questions it might be a good idea to talk to one of your fellow workers about your feelings. Odds are others feel similarly. Perhaps it would be a good topic to discuss at a staff meeting. That would allow you the opportunity for you and your fellow workers to acknowledge your feelings about the client and to develop strategies to be able to continue to work therapeutically with them.

CHAPTER 19
COMMUNICATION WITH A DISTURBED INDIVIDUAL

General Attitude and Approaches:
A. Attitude or feeling state:

- Control your own behavior. Remain calm ("mirror calm").
- Be non-judgmental.
- Avoid threatening words or actions.
- Don't take insults personally.
- Do not enter a power struggle.
- Use "soft focus" eye contact and an expression that says "I'm your friend, not your enemy".
- Show concern without anger.
- Be in firm but kindly control.
- Be empathetic. (Remember "Hurt People, Hurt People"). Show that you have listened and understood how the individual feels. "I heard you say..."; "As I understand it..."; "I know it is difficult for you, how can I make it easier?"
- Show respect, if only because he/she is a human being and all human beings are entitled to respect. Show the person you are for him/her, not neutral and not against him/her.

- Be genuine. Don't respond in an institutionalized or stereotyped professional manner. Try to affect an open, spontaneous interaction style. Use your own language and avoid buzz words that might anger the person e.g. "It is our policy..."
- Be concrete. Deal with the individual in and with specific, concrete feelings, behaviors and directions. Do not be vague. Do not lie.
- Recognize and reinforce steps to regain control. Use positive gestures and language.
- Trust your intuition and feelings. Ask the person if you are correct. For example, "I have the feeling you are upset because your daughter couldn't visit today. Am I right or wrong about that?"
- Be aware of personal responses to aggressive behavior. Caregivers who project their own feelings of rage and fear onto the impaired will overestimate the potential for violence and resort to excessive use of restraints, physical or chemical.
- Heed inner dialogue (awareness of counter-transference reactions).
- Avoid the "saviors" or "macho" attitude in an effort to live up to expectations of on-lookers or to compensate for personal fears.

B. Speech

- Use simple, concrete, positive statements. Say what you want them **to do** not **what you don't want them to do**. For example, "Please sit over here" instead of "Don't pace in the dining room."
- State instructions or questions one at a time. When they can respond appropriately, they are regaining control.
- Keep voice volume appropriate for distance and the person's ability to hear. Raising the voice raises the pitch. This is the hardest range for the elderly to hear.
- Use a smooth supportive tone.

- Use normal speech rhythm. Speaking too fast, too slowly or in a jumpy excited manner can irritate the person and escalate the problem. Address persons by name, e.g. "John"
- Pay attention to the response. Do not assume your message is understood.
- Do not use jargon.
- Avoid giving advice.
- Listen and learn, open and active listening (nod and "yes, yes"). What does the client see as the problem and what do they expect of you?
- Use silence and restatement to clarify the message.
- Ask questions to seek information, a favor or to distract the person.
- Avoid sarcastic or insulting remarks. Be careful of using humor. When in doubt, don't try to be funny. Humor is a high risk, high gain technique.
- Reassure acting-out and frightened individuals that you, the care-giver, did not intend to be a threat.
- Telling aggressive people their behavior frightens, worries or upsets you can be appropriate. They may not see their behavior this way and may attempt to change it.
- Asking individuals who are aware of their aggressive urges to tell you when something you do or say makes them angry may defuse a touchy situation.
- Verbal abuse is not always a safety valve and may aggravate assault.

C. Non-verbal messages

- Be aware of non-verbal communication. A person cannot "not communicate."
- Avoid exaggerated gestures which may startle or threaten.
- Reduce nervous mannerisms and avoid over-activity. You will appear in control even though you may not feel that way.

- Portray a confident non-anxious manner.
- Keep your hands in view and not behind the back or in the pockets. The person may believe you are hiding something.
- Approach with the palms open. This is the handshake or welcoming position.
- Honor "personal space". Remember the variables involved include the sex, size, familiarity and the speed of the approaching helper.
- Remember this distance may double or triple when a person is in a crisis state.
- Use the "tactical interview stance". Standing at least one leg length distance from the client (about 3 feet) and turned approximately 45 degrees to the side with the hands in plain sight is less threatening and offers individuals a "perceived" route of escape. Keep hands open and above waist line. Standing squarely face to face is issuing a challenge and is also unsafe.
- Avoid standing over people who are upset. Use eye level. Use increased distance to approach eye level.
- Isolate the situation.

1. **Empathic Listening (an active process to discern what a person is saying)**

- Don't be judgmental.
- Don't ignore or fake attention.
- Carefully listen to what a person is really saying.
- Use silence and restatement to clarify messages.
- Reflection can be used to clarify.

Listening Versus Really Hearing

Give others a chance to choose their own course of action

PROTECT YOURSELF NOW!

...

THERE IS A TENDENCY AMONG LISTENERS TO TRY TO RESCUE A person with problems and pull them out of negative situations. People don't really want that. They just want to discuss what is on their minds and reach their own conclusions.

REALLY LISTENING PHASES ARE:

"You seem to think..."

"You sound like..."

"You appear to be..."

"As I understand it, you..."

A CONSTANT BOMBARDMENT OF QUESTIONS CAN DISRUPT communication and be a barrier to conversation. Commands will have the same effect and many of them are impossible to follow, anyway.

"Stop feeling depressed..."

"Don't be so upset..."

"Don't think about it..."

"Stop worrying..."

COMMENTS THAT SEEM THREATENING WILL END A CONVERSATION AS quickly as changing the subject or not paying attention.

"YOU HAD BETTER STOP FEELING SAD..."

"You had better stop feeling... or I will..."

CHAPTER 20
SECTION TWO SUMMARY:

In Section Two we explored the criteria for conducting a risk assessment for workplace violence. We were challenged to consider how we personally view working with potentially violent individuals. This would be a good topic to discuss with your coworkers at break time or at a staff meeting.

We were then introduced to techniques to utilize when communicating with a disturbed individual.

SECTION THREE WILL INTRODUCE US TO THE NATURE OF CRISES AND provide examples of the characteristics of crisis-prone individuals in a Quick List. We will then learn how to identify events that can trigger a crisis response. We then move on to identifying and expanding upon the four levels of a crisis. Specific attitudes or approaches to be used in each of the four levels of a crisis are introduced.

WE WILL THEN DIFFERENTIATE SUPPORTIVE AND DIRECTIVE approaches to take with a disturbed individual and the appropriate time to use them. This is followed by techniques to handle verbal aggression.

From there, we move in to exploring how our body language works for or against us in resolving a crisis. Physical interventions are discussed. We focus on the psychological reactions experienced by an individual in crisis.

Techniques for utilizing a team approach to resolve a workplace crisis are explored.

There is always paperwork to be completed in any unusual situation. We will explore the legal aspects of documenting, post incident. Then, we will move into exploring post incident debriefing techniques. Tips on contacting emergency responders i.e. police, fire & ambulance will be provided.

How we as individuals handle a crisis will be explored. Do we stay or do we run? Section Three concludes with several case studies from my experience to illustrate the chapter's content.

∽

SECTION THREE:
WHAT IS A CRISIS?

CHAPTER 21
WHAT IS A CRISIS?

AWARENESS

Crisis results from stress and tension in a person's life. Stress is the element in crisis development. As stress mounts to unusual proportions and the individual's coping skills become increasingly ineffective, the potential for crisis occurs.

THE NATURE OF CRISES

PROTECT YOURSELF NOW!

. . .

A CRISIS OVERRIDES AN INDIVIDUAL'S NORMAL PSYCHOLOGICAL AND biological coping mechanisms. Several features of critical incidents account for the overwhelming and bewildering nature of a crisis. As people grow and develop, they continually meet new demands. These demands could be intellectual, employment-related, economic, or rooted in relationships with other people.

INDIVIDUALS MEET THESE DEMANDS AND PRACTICE RESOLVING THEM so often that they form coping mechanisms, or "cognitive maps," to deal with them. These maps assist people who face a potential problem to categorize it, determine the resources needed to overcome it, choose a solution, and set a goal for the problem's resolution.

OCCASIONALLY, HOWEVER, INDIVIDUALS CONFRONT SITUATIONS THEY have seldom or never encountered in the past. As a result, they have not developed adequate coping mechanisms to deal with them. These crises leave individuals feeling overwhelmed and powerless. For many people, these crises cause their heightened emotions to impair their ability to think rationally.

AS A CONSEQUENCE OF FEELING POWERLESS AND HELPLESS, individuals may experience extreme levels of physiological arousal in the form of anxiety --- the natural human response to threat and danger. This anxiety serves to disrupt further their ability to think clearly. Consequently, when individuals face a crisis, their increased levels of arousal interfere with attempts to cope with an already incomprehensible circumstance.

DURING SITUATIONS OF CRISIS, PEOPLE SPONTANEOUSLY TURN TO others for comfort, support, understanding, and protection. Some research suggests that people possess a biological need for attachment. Crises, however, have the potential to disconnect individuals from necessary sources of support. When the cry for attachment and support is not answered due to others' misunderstanding of, fear of, anger with, disappointment in, or disagreement with the individual in crisis, that person feels utterly abandoned.

THE ABSENCE OF SUPPORT DURING A CRISIS REPRESENTS THE LOSS OF the primary human coping resource. Without the sense of security provided by others, the troubled individual's already extreme state of physiological arousal is exacerbated further. As a growing feeling of despair sets in, the person feels unable to escape the crisis. When all roads back to equilibrium seem blocked, the individual's ability to cope becomes overwhelmed.

AS EVERY ATTEMPT TO DEAL WITH THE PERCEIVED THREAT seemingly meets with failure, the individual learns to do nothing. This state of "learned helplessness" is characterized by constricted thinking and an inability to see even the most obvious solutions. Instead, the individual focuses on moment-to-moment survival. This shift in thinking only complicates the individual's situation, serving to undermine the sense of personal competence and effectiveness while increasing anxiety even more.

CRISIS INTERVENTION/MANAGEMENT IS AN ATTEMPT TO DEAL quickly with an immediate problem. Often it requires providing for victims that which the victims cannot provide for themselves. This can include a physical or emotional crutch to lean on, and even direction by the intervener at a time in the victim's life when self-direction may be impossible.

Anatomy of a Crisis

The following four levels have been identified in a crisis:

Anxiety Level

Defensive Level

Acting Out Physically

Tension Reduction Stage*

* You need to be aware that this stage may occur at any level in the crisis.

Based on information from The Crisis Prevention Institute

Indicators That Can Characterize A Crisis-Prone Person

ALIENATION FROM LASTING AND MEANINGFUL PERSONAL relationships

- Inability to use life support systems such as family, friends, and social groups
- Difficulty in learning from experience; the individual continues to make the same mistakes
- A history of previously experienced crises that have not been effectively resolved

- A history of mental disorder or severe emotional imbalance
- Feelings of low self-esteem
- Provocative, impulsive behavior resulting from unresolved inner conflict
- A history of poor marital relationships
- Excessive use of drugs, including alcohol abuse
- Marginal income
- Lack of regular, fulfilling work
- Unusual or frequent physical injuries
- Frequent changes in residence

- Frequent encounters with the law
- An accident in the home
- An automobile accident, with or without injury
- Being arrested, appearing in court
- Changes in a job situation and income involving either promotion or demotion
- Change in school status

CHAPTER 22
INDICATORS THAT CAN CHARACTERIZE A CRISIS-PRONE PERSON

Alienation from lasting and meaningful personal relationships

- Inability to use life support systems such as family, friends, and social groups
- Difficulty in learning from experience; the individual continues to make the same mistakes
- A history of previously experienced crises that have not been effectively resolved
- A history of mental disorder or severe emotional imbalance
- Feelings of low self-esteem
- Provocative, impulsive behavior resulting from unresolved inner conflict
- A history of poor marital relationships
- Excessive use of drugs, including alcohol abuse
- Marginal income
- Lack of regular, fulfilling work
- Unusual or frequent physical injuries

- Frequent changes in residence
- Frequent encounters with the law

CHAPTER 23
EVENTS THAT CAN PRECIPITATE A CRISIS

- An accident in the home
- An automobile accident, with or without injury
- Being arrested, appearing in court
- Changes in a job situation and income involving either promotion or demotion
- Change in school status
- Death of a significant person in one's life
- Divorce or separation
- A delinquency episode either (in childhood or adulthood; skipping school or running away from home; in adulthood: failure to pay debts)
- Entry into school
- Abortion or out-of-wedlock pregnancy
- Physical illness
- Acute episodes of mental disorder
- Retirement
- Natural disasters
- Sexual difficulties
- Major change in living conditions

- Gaining a new family member (for example, through birth, adoption, or parents or adult children moving in)
- Dealing with a blended family
- Foreclosure on a mortgage or loan
- Actual or impending loss of something significant in one's life

lthough a particular stressful situation may not induce crisis, a combination of several such stressful events may push the individual to the crisis point.

BACK TO THE ANATOMY OF A CRISIS...

CHAPTER 24
SPECIFIC STAFF ATTITUDES OR APPROACHES TO BE USED IN THE FOUR LEVELS OF A CRISIS

Definition: **Nonviolent Crisis Intervention** - is a non-harmful behavior management system designed to aid staff in maintaining the best possible care and welfare of agitated or out-of-control individuals... even during their most violent moments.

IN ANY CRISIS DEVELOPMENT SITUATION, THERE ARE FOUR DISTINCT and identifiable behavior levels. Each behavior level demands a specific staff response to provide the maximum chance of defusing the crisis development.

- Anxiety Level:

DEFINITION: ANXIETY - AN UNEASINESS OF TENSION RESULTING from anticipation or danger or source which is unknown. In this stage you will observe an escalation of their anxiety. Many symptoms of anxiety were previously identified as disturbed behavior.

- Pacing
- Muttering
- Swearing
- Exaggerated Movements (quick and erratic)
- Staring
- Avoiding Eye Contact
- Eyes Narrowed
- Darting eyes
- Looking Angry
- Body Tensed- neck, jaw, arms
- Fist Clenched
- Restlessness
- Withdrawal
- Rocking
- Banging Objects
- Restlessness
- Wringing hands
- Picking at something
- Talking loudly, quickly or in a demanding voice

GOAL: TO LOWER ANXIETY LEVEL TO CALM.

To restore equilibrium (lower anxiety, guilt and tension and provide emotional support).

IN THIS STAGE A ***SUPPORTIVE*** ATTITUDE IS MOST EFFECTIVE.

CARRY OUT ALL INTERVENTIONS IN A CALM MANNER.

- Display genuine interest.
- Listen actively and with empathy.
- Encourage talking using open-ended questions. Encouraging helps counteract the sense of helplessness & hopelessness and gives more confidence to try new ways of facing the situation.

DEAL WITH THE PERSON'S FEELINGS. ALLOW THEM TO VENTILATE. Let the individual "get it off their chest."

Provide reassurance. Tell the person that anxiety is normal in a crisis and that other people frequently experience similar feelings.

Be actively friendly.

Use silence when appropriate.

Make a verbal contract.

Respect personal space.

Go "beyond the call of duty." Demonstrate your active concern by doing something extra — it may say that you care about his/her situation.

- **Defensive Level (anger, hostility)**

THE INDIVIDUAL IS BECOMING BELLIGERENT, NONCOMPLIANT AND challenging, aroused by a real or supposed wrong. He may begin to lose rational control. Yelling, refusals, relentless questioning, name calling and intimidating statements may occur. The client might be under the influence of delusional ideation or may be receiving faulty messages from hallucinatory thoughts.

IF THE CLIENT IS LUCID, AT THIS POINT, THEY ARE NOT TOTALLY IN control of their life and may feel panic resulting from this realization.

Client may flail about emotionally, verbally, or even physically as they experience this lack of control.

A ***DIRECTIVE*** ATTITUDE/APPROACH IS BEST IN THIS STAGE:

GOAL: TO LOWER ANGER TO ANXIETY LEVEL.

To restore equilibrium by helping the person find new alternatives.

- Enter the crisis scene cautiously. Approach any crisis situation slowly and carefully. Caution at this point can prevent unnecessary grief. Take a moment to mentally compute what you: hear, see, smell, feel, sense, touch.
- Communicate your expectations in a clear, concise Elicit reasons for refusal: offering options/choices and a specific time to decide.
- Try to align yourself with the individual by finding a common goal. e.g. "We both want to find a solution to this problem?"
- Give advice. Provide guidance in choosing a course of action or assuming a new role.
- Provide choices. Offer two different courses of action (A or B) that lead to restoration of equilibrium, or one course of action the person can take by him/herself or with help.
- Maintain focus on the issue at hand.
- Set realistic, enforceable limits and advise the person of consequences of all options; stating positive consequences first.
- Avoid entering the individual's personal space. If possible, give extra personal space.
- Avoid confrontative or threatening gestures. Remember the person's perceptions may be inaccurate.
- Your hand movements are important. Use a palm up position if possible. Avoid hands in pockets, hands behind back, folded

arms, clenched fists or fist-like motions, hands on hips, and pointing fingers.
- Do not touch a person who is in the defensive stage as this may stimulate them to become physically aggressive.
- Maintain eye contact without staring or moving eyes too frequently.
- Be aware of the powerful impact of your own voice tone. Our tone, volume, and rate of speech accounts for 85-90% of our communication. How we ***say it*** is very important!
- Refrain from talking over the person when they are yelling and/or swearing. Deliver a concise verbal intervention when the person takes a breath or stops their verbal abuse.
- Do not argue.
- . Do not use jargon or lengthy explanations.
- Isolate the behavior by removing others from the room or, if possible, move the aggressive individual to a private place to continue the conversation. Ensure that you have a clear exit route should the person escalate to the next stage of acting out.

CHAPTER 25
LEVEL TWO -- HOSTILITY (MORE ADVANCED)

Definition: **Hostility**- A verbal or threatening physical response toward the destruction or damage of a person or object, interpreted as a source of frustration or threat.

GOAL: TO LOWER HOSTILITY TO THE ANGER LEVEL.

To restore equilibrium by assuming control.

- Warn. Clearly state the consequences of a given course of action.
- Set Limits. Clearly state the boundaries of behavior that you will allow.
- Give Directives. Firmly tell the individual what you want him/her to do.

YOUR NONVERBAL BEHAVIOR BECOMES VERY IMPORTANT DURING this defensive stage.

CHAPTER 26
INTERVENTION PROCESS
HORIZONTAL VIOLENCE & BULLYING

Review Incident
Gain Control
Find Help
Plan for Action
Document
Confront
Formal Written Complaint

∼

CHAPTER 27
GUIDELINES FOR DEALING WITH VERBAL AGGRESSION

Action

S tay calm.

- Take all threats of violence toward you seriously. People often follow through with the threats that they make.
- Maintain a distance of about three feet. Increase this if the person is agitated, (fidgeting, pacing, prolonged staring) or verbally loud.
- Ensure that the aggressive person has a clear path to the exit.
- Speak slowly, clearly. Don't raise your voice in response to the client's loud voice. "Please put the chair down now." ***not***

"C'mon now, let me have the chair you're going to hurt somebody and I'll have to call the police."
- Keep you posture receptive. For example, keep your arms uncrossed and with your hands out of pockets visible above your waist, palms open; stand at an angle.
- Set gentle limits. "Lower your voice." "Slow down." "Let's sit down and talk."
- Don't set limits you cannot enforce. (This may actually increase aggression.)
- Above all, show respect. Don't talk down to the client. Emphasize you want to help and you are trying to help.

INTERVENING WITH A CLIENT WHO IS VERBALLY AGGRESSIVE CAN BE very stressful. You may find it helpful to use the **Stop Strategy** to help gather your thoughts.

CHAPTER 28
STOP STRATEGY

S**low Down** Try to slow your words and your movements. Put yourself in slow motion to help calm your feelings. If you can step out of the situation, take three slow deep breaths and count slowly to 10 before returning to the situation.

T THINK ABOUT WHAT IS HAPPENING ASK yourself: HOW DO I feel? Is this out of proportion? Could I do this later when I'm feeling less rushed? Can someone else give me a better perspective on this?

O OPTIONS OPEN YOUR EYES TO ALTERNATIVES. HOW CAN THIS BE done differently? Seek ideas from other staff.

P PLAN PLAN TO HAVE SOME TIME TO YOURSELF. IT IS IMPOSSIBLE to be a giving and caring person if you are overtired and overwhelmed. Make time for regular daily activity, such as a brisk walk, and get adequate rest.

PROTECT YOURSELF NOW!

~

CHAPTER 29
ACTING OUT PHYSICALLY

Definition: Aggression - A hostile action directed towards a person or thing.

When a client physically acts out, you may see the following focus for their aggression:

- Environment e.g. slamming doors, pushing or throwing furniture
- Self e.g. removing life-saving medical equipment such as IVs
- Others e.g. striking out, grabbing

A *DIRECTIVE* ATTITUDE/APPROACH CONTINUES TO BE THE BEST and should include the following:

* THIS MAY BE WHEN YOU HAVE TO CALL FOR HELP OR LEAVE!

. . .

Goal:

- To lower aggression level to the hostility/anger levels.
- To protect physical structures (building, furniture, equipment, etc.)
- Take physical control to protect the client, visitors and staff from injury or harm.
- To restore equilibrium by assuming control.

- Create a plan of action with the resources that you have available (a show of force can be reassuring to the person who is out of control and will, in most cases, not require physical intervention.)
- The team leader, the only person speaking to the aggressive individual, should communicate calmly, directly, and reassuringly.* Offer medication if this is indicated and there is a physician's order. If it is refused, offer a choice of oral or intramuscular.
- Reinforce with the client the expectations and limits to their behavior you had previously communicated to them.
- The first approach to this stage continues to be verbal intervention to de-escalate the aggressive behavior. Build bridges, maintain a verbal link between yourself and the client during a physical/chemical restraint, so when the patient calms down, an effective verbal intervention can continue.
- If possible remove the client from the source of the stress.
- Remove all other clients, visitors etc. from the immediate area. (an audience can add an undesirable element to the client's distress)
- If the aggression turns physical and is directed towards you, use self-defense techniques to extricate yourself if necessary.

Remember to use the least amount of force required!)*

Remember a non-violent intervention is desired!

The role of the Team Leader in a crisis will be explored later.

CHAPTER 30
TYPES OF ASSAULT

T he most *frequent modes* of assault are punching, scratching, biting, physical resistance (such as pushing and struggling) and kicking.

The most COMMON TARGETS are the arms & hands and the most frequent injuries lacerations, bruising and sprains.

CHAPTER 31
THE EFFECTS OF HELPER BODY LANGUAGE IN RESOLVING A CRISIS

AWARENESS

- body language must be congruent with words spoken
- do not move hands and arms around unnecessarily
- do not use hand gestures as they may be misunderstood
- do not make sudden movements, especially in the direction of the client
- do not turn your back on an agitated client
- remain calm

PROTECT YOURSELF NOW!

CHAPTER 32
PHYSICAL INTERVENTIONS/SELF-DEFENSE TECHNIQUES

Despite, your best verbal interventions the client may escalate to the point that physical intervention is necessary. It is beyond the scope of this book to provide and illustrate proper techniques of applying physical interventions. A non-violent intervention is required.

Principles include:

- using the least amount of force required to defuse any given situation
- the focus is on defense not offence i.e. neutralizing the attack not the attacker
- effective self-defense techniques decrease the severity of client and staff injury
- using your head, is the best defense (i.e. strategic thinking, not as a battering ram!)
- the techniques must be reviewed and practiced regularly to be of use to you

When intervening with an agitated person, the concept of personal space should be front and foremost in your mind. A face-to-face, eye-to-eye, toe-to-toe would likely be interpreted as a "challenge" position and tends to escalate an individual in a crisis situation.

∼

CHAPTER 33
PERSONAL SPACE

AWARENESS

Invasion or encroachment of personal space tends to heighten or escalate anxiety.

- Think of a person having a circle three feet in diameter around them.
- Invading an individual's "personal space" during a crisis

development situation tends to minimize your chances of defusing the situation and maximize the chances of escalating the situation.
- Any intrusion into this area may result in a client striking out.
- Intrusions of personal space may be unconscious e.g., a helper attempting to hug or touch a disturbed person to comfort or console them. ***

Proactive Tip: As healthcare providers, many of us want to console our clients when they are in distress. While sitting on their bed and holding our child might be successful in reducing their anxiety, in a clinical setting it could have the opposite effect. Agitated clients can easily misunderstand your motive or intent and lash out at you. If you are within that three foot personal zone, you are placing yourself in hazard.

A "Defensive Stance" is recommended when speaking and intervening with an agitated client. (previously mentioned as a Tactical Interview Stance)

- Feet placed 15-18 inches apart (allows a solid base to balance)
- Knees slightly bent allowing movement and flexing (allows for better pivoting, and shock absorption)
- Arms at side free to move, not in pockets or holding something (allows free movement of hands for defensive actions)
- Body facing slightly away from the client, not directly facing (allows for defense of vulnerable areas of groin and abdomen)
- Distance of at least three feet away from the client

Benefits of the Defensive stance:

- It does not encroach upon the individual's personal space

- It avoids a challenging position
- It improves staff's personal safety i.e. reduces the chance of injury

If you are being restrained:

- the element of surprise is in your favor
- use the least amount of force needed to extricate yourself
- when released, move out of the way as the attacker may apply another hold

How Client May React to Physical Intervention:

- further escalation
- submission
- suicidal ideation
- physiological decompensation (heart attack etc.)
- physical injuries

CHAPTER 34
TENSION REDUCTION STAGE (RECOVERY)

Assess the client for the following behaviors signalling tension reduction:

- Reduced energy level
- Withdrawal
- Regaining rational control
- Remorse
- Guilt
- Fear
- Embarrassment
- Sadness

YOU NEED TO BE AWARE THAT THIS STAGE MAY OCCUR AT ANY LEVEL in the crisis.

* Depression is a danger during this stage.

. . .

Specific interventions are dependent upon the stage of crisis that tension reduction occurs in.

In the Tension Reduction Stage, once again, a ***SUPPORTIVE*** attitude is most effective.

- Carry out all interventions in a calm manner
- Display genuine interest
- Listen actively and with empathy
- Encourage talking using open-ended questions
- Deal with the person's feelings
- Be actively friendly
- Use silence when appropriate

The 'triggers' or reasons for losing control, plus alternative ways of behaving/coping should be explored to prevent a repeat occurrence.

Suggest alternative acceptable behaviour and establish an agreement, or contract for behaviour change.

Consequences must match the severity of the behaviour, i.e. withdrawal of services, limitation of privileges, pressing legal charges.

Teach appropriate methods of expressing emotions.

Discuss relaxation techniques to defuse negative emotions before they result in aggressive behaviour.

Identify witnesses to the aggressive behaviour and allow them to vent their feelings.

*Note: People will not necessarily go through all these stages, and they will not necessarily go through them in this order. For instance, someone may go from anxiety to recovery without becoming physically aggressive. In most cases, physical aggression is preceded by the early stages of behaviours.

. . .

THE "TRIGGERS" OR REASONS FOR LOSING CONTROL, PLUS alternative ways of behaving/coping should be explored to prevent a repeat occurrence.

Suggest alternative acceptable behavior and establish an agreement, or contract for behavior change.

Consequences must match the severity of the behavior, i.e. withdrawal of services, limitation of privileges, pressing legal charges.

Teach appropriate methods of expressing emotions.

Discuss relaxation techniques to defuse negative emotions before they result in aggressive behavior.

Identify witnesses to the aggressive behavior and allow them to vent their feelings.

*NOTE: PEOPLE WILL NOT NECESSARILY GO THROUGH ALL THESE stages, and they will not necessarily go through them in this order. For instance, someone may go from anxiety to recovery without becoming physically aggressive. In most cases, physical aggression is preceded by the early stages of behaviors.

CHAPTER 35
RECOGNIZING A PERSON IN CRISIS

AWARENESS

R ecognition depends upon:

Intervener's awareness of what the victim is communicating verbally and nonverbally

Intervener's sensing capabilities

. . .

Different people may indicate crisis in different ways:

a. Crying out, exploding, verbalizing

b. Withdrawal, depression, or both

If possible, the intervener should obtain information from family and friends about the victim's pre-crisis behavior and note disruptions in previous behavior, as well as modes of ineffective functioning.

Profile of a person in crisis:

- **Bewilderment:** "I never felt this way before."
- **Danger:** "I'm so nervous and scared."
- **Confusion:** "I can't think clearly."
- **Impasse:** "I feel stuck; nothing I do helps."
- **Apathy:** "Nothing can help me."
- **Desperation:** "I've got to do something."
- **Helplessness:** "I can't take care of myself."
- **Urgency:** "I need help now!!!!!!!"
- **Discomfort:** "I feel miserable, restless, and unsettled."

At this point, the victim is not totally in control of life and feels the panic resulting from this realization. Victims may flail about emotionally, verbally, or even physically as they experience this lack of control.

CHAPTER 36
COMMON SIGNS & SYMPTOMS OF PSYCHOLOGICAL REACTIONS TO CRISIS

Emotional:

Anticipatory anxiety; inadequacy; generalized anxiety; feeling overwhelmed; shock; anger; denial; irritability; insecurity; fatigue; uncertainty; fear; despair; survivor; guilt; feeling out of control; grief; outrage; numbness; helplessness; panic; frustration.

Cognitive:

Confusion; poor attention span; poor concentration; flashbacks; loss of trust; difficulties in decision making; nightmares.

Behavioral:

Withdrawal; sleep disturbances; angry outbursts; change in activity; change in appetite; increased fatigue; excessive use of sick leave; alcohol or drug abuse; irritability; difficulty functioning at normal ability level; antisocial acts; frequent visits to physician for nonspecific complaints; anger at God; loss of desire to attend religious services; regression; crying; change in communications; preoccupation with the crisis to the exclusion of other areas of life; diminished job performance; unresponsiveness; hysterical reactions.

PROTECT YOURSELF NOW!

CHAPTER 37
PROBLEM SOLVING METHOD TO DEAL WITH CRISIS SITUATIONS

AWARENESS

1. Assess 2. Plan 3. Implement 4. Evaluate

1. **Assessment:**

THE INITIAL ASSESSMENT IS EXTREMELY IMPORTANT. WHENEVER possible, try to observe the individual's behavior in a variety of situations. When the individual's behavior is becoming aggressive, assessments must be made quickly.

USE INFORMATION FROM ALL AVAILABLE SOURCES, E.G. FAMILY, clinical records, coworkers. Be aware of behavioral clues and predictors of disturbed behavior. Assessment should lead to Problem Identification and Priority Setting.

1. **Planning:** The planning stage is composed of three phases:

1. Immediate Interventions
2. Short Term Planning
3. Long Term Planning

ONCE THE PROBLEMS HAVE BEEN IDENTIFIED, THE NEXT STEP IS TO establish goals or objectives and to plan how to best achieve them.

CHAPTER 38
USE A TEAM INTERVENTION

AWARENESS

team intervention provides:

- Safety

- Professionalism
- Support

TEAM INTERVENTION IS THE BEST APPROACH TO USE IN ANY CRISIS development. Staff should always begin an intervention utilizing the least restrictive method of controlling the aggressive person.

The objective is to resolve any crisis situation with the least amount of conflict. By utilizing therapeutic intervention techniques throughout the entire intervention, staff can provide the best possible care and welfare, safely and securely for all involved.

WHO SHOULD BE A TEAM LEADER?

1. First person on the scene.

2. Team member with confidence.

3. Team member who knows the client.

4. In many cases, (automatically) the person in charge.

COMMENT: WITHIN THE HEALTHCARE FIELD THERE ARE SEVERAL variations of the term *"team."* For the purpose of this manual we will use the description of two or more people working together. One member of the team may or may not have authority over the other(s). A team may develop as a spontaneous reaction to a situation. An example may be that some of your fellow workers are off the unit having their lunch. You are all part of the "team" for the day. Now let's say that while they are away, a crisis occurs. A new team, from those workers remaining on the unit, would evolve to deal with the crisis. The team leader for the new team may not have any authority related to their position but by virtue of being the most experienced worker or the most knowledgeable of the client involved, might assume the role of team leader.

. . .

In many clinical settings there is a designated person called the Team Leader or Charge Nurse. They would probably receive financial compensation for this additional responsibility. This responsibility and resulting accountability could cause problems for them should they choose to delegate their authority to another or abdicate their responsibilities to another. If they choose to defer to a more experienced colleague or perhaps a more confident one, they should still maintain an active role in the process. They may be held liable should the intervention be ineffective.

In some facilities, the staff person involved is advised to assess his or her own "rational control" and decide whether it is appropriate for them to be team leader. In other facilities, the staff member originally involved is encouraged not to participate in the team at all. If the individual has been assaulted, if at all possible, they should not be involved with the subsequent intervention.

Questions a Team Leader should consider in planning intervention:

- What exactly is the problem? Why is the client behaving in this matter? Can the situation be resolved rather quickly or do we need to prepare a plan?
- What do we hope to achieve in this situation? What is the goal? What is our priority?

What might happen if we ignore or don't take action in this situation?

- If we do take action, might it set into motion another event that we hadn't considered?
- What might our peers do in a similar situation?

- Has the client been in a similar situation before? How did they behave at that time?
- Has a similar situation or event occurred previously? How was it handled then? Was a plan implemented to help in this situation? If so, where might it be? How did the client respond at that time?
- How will our actions affect the client?
- What are the capabilities/skills/experience of my fellow staff? Are they able to perform the functions that I assign them? Do they have any specific limitations?
- If this plan fails do I have a back-up plan?
- Have all safety features been taken into consideration? How do I provide for the safety of other clients, visitors etc., while we intervene?
- Are there any Policies or Procedures that would influence or determine the action that we take?
- Am I able to call anyone for help? How long will take for help to arrive?
- Are all staff clear of what their roles are prior to intervening?

Action

DUTIES OF THE TEAM LEADER: IT IS VERY IMPORTANT TO THE team outcome that one person takes a clear leadership role. The team leader's role includes the following:

- **Assess the situation (determine what steps are necessary):**

1. what happened?
2. what has been done so far?
3. what action is required by the team

* **Most important!** Carry out all interventions in a calm manner.

- **Plan the intervention with the team:**
- ensure that every member of the team knows their role in the intervention (if you are a football fan, think of the team huddle that the Quarterback uses to determine the strategy of the next play)
- assign which body part each member of the team is to restrain should this be necessary

- **Direct the team or cue them:**
- ensure activity and situation in the immediate area is kept at a minimum
- ensure patients, staff not directly involved and visitors are removed from the area
- obtain backup if required and available i.e. security staff, police
- ensure all members of the team remove objects which may damage or cause injury, for example: eyeglasses, pens, watches, pagers, scissors

- **Communicate with the client (only one person should talk to the client to avoid confusion):**
  - be sure all staff are aware of this

- **Decide if and when it is appropriate to move from verbal to physical intervention:**
  - give clear direction to the team if you wish them to move forward and restrain the individual (some Emergency Response Teams [ERT] utilize a code phrase to indicate the team leader's direction to apply physical restraint. One example is "Okay, you win!")

- **Follow-up the intervention by conducting a quick debriefing of the incident and completing the incident form.**
  - this allows the staff to reduce their own tension after the incident
  - the person in charge of the shift should lead the debrief

AWARENESS

Potential Problems Encountered by Team Leaders

Proactive Tip: Sometimes internal power struggles can get in the way of constructive leadership. The team may not agree with your decision. You may find yourself demanding that they follow your suggestions or conceding to the group's decision. If you are the senior person or designated as "in charge" you may be responsible should there be deleterious results from your choice of action (or inaction).

1. **Implementation:** This stage, of course, is to put your plan into action. It is sometimes helpful to have a Plan B in place should plan A be unsuccessful. (Plan C & D might be helpful as well!)

1. **Evaluation:** The fourth stage of a problem solving method to deal with crisis situations. This should take place while you are intervening as well as after your chosen intervention has been implemented. As mentioned above, it may be necessary to quickly enact an alternate plan of action.

Whether you were successful or unsuccessful, there are valuable lessons to be learned from any situation. However, before you evaluate the situation, it is imperative that you document the event.

CHAPTER 39
LEGAL ASPECTS AND DOCUMENTATION

Awareness

Reports should be written immediately after the event by persons involved. Every organization has a different system for reporting. It is important that you are aware of the reporting procedure for your setting. Necessary documentation may include: nursing/interdisciplinary progress notes; Workers Compensation Board Incident Report; facility specific Unusual Incident Report;

Facility Licensing report. It is generally recommended that you keep your own private notes of the situation should you need them for future reference. However, it is not suggested that you photocopy reports that you file as they are considered belonging to your employer.

Reports must be:

- written by the individuals involved
- accurate
- concise
- legible
- in chronological order
- dated & signed
- once you have written on the report, do not erase
- use only acceptable abbreviations
- incident reports should be written (and signed) immediately after the event by the persons involved

ISSUES TO EXAMINE IN THE DOCUMENTATION ARE:

- Time and duration of the incident.
- Who was involved?
- What happened?
- What precipitated the incident?
- Description of behavior preceding the incident, during and after, including any threats. Use descriptive, non-judgmental terms to describe the behavior.
- De-escalating techniques used and their effectiveness.
- Type and duration of physical restraints used.
- Effect of physical and/or chemical intervention.
- Follow-up communication with the person re the incident.
- What was the outcome?

REPORTS NEED TO BE WORDED TO ENSURE THAT THE IMPLICATION IS not that the health care workers were at fault. Instead of asking, "What could you have done to prevent this incident?"... ask "What events or circumstances precipitated the incident?"

∼

CHAPTER 40
INCIDENT REVIEW & POST EVENT DEBRIEFING

These two actions tend to get combined together but actually serve different purposes.

Post event debriefing is an informal meeting with the staff involved in the incident immediately following the incident. Its purpose is to make sure everybody is okay. People respond to critical incidents in different ways. We discuss some of those reactions in greater detail in Chapter Six.

Post event debriefing is the time to advise those involved in the incident of the availability of employee assistance programs, if available, should they require professional help in processing their involvement in the crisis. It is also the time to ensure that the proper follow-up documentation will take place.

On the other hand, an *incident review* should be done post incident, either informally by those involved in the incident or later, conducted formally by the supervisor. It can be scheduled at a mutually beneficial time and need not take place immediately after the incident. This is where we ask the who, what, where, how & why questions.

Questions to ask.

What happened?

What was happening prior to and following the incident?

What could have been done to avert the incident?

What was well done during the implementation of the action plan?

What could be done differently, next time?

What can we learn from this situation? (client, staffing, ward organization)

How can we prevent a similar situation from reoccurring?

Proactive Tip: To prevent a similar incident from reoccurring, it is necessary to be proactive in acting upon the lessons that were learned during the incident review. Depending on the individual involved, there is often value in interviewing them, after the crisis has been resolved, to see if they are open to developing techniques to prevent the event from reoccurring.

A precautionary note is warranted here as well. The intent of an incident review is to find the root causes and to learn from them, not to affix blame to someone. Some organizations, unfortunately, continue to play the "blame game."

The following sections: A Safety Check, Prevention and Management of Aggression Checklist, Actions to take with specific client groups, all deal with preventative techniques.

Some incidents can be psychologically traumatic to the participants. Another type of incident review will be explored later in this book under the heading of ***Critical Incident Debriefing***.

A Safety Check (to be done on an ongoing basis)

Are precautions communicated to all staff including new and relief staff?

Does the off-going shift report *potential* or *actual* client disturbed behavior to the oncoming shift?

Are support staff i.e. housekeepers, maintenance, laundry-workers advised of potentially hazardous situations?

Are *routine* policies & procedures safe?

Is the physical environment relatively safe?

Does new-hire orientation and staff education stress safety?

Are staff from all professions, plus administration, supportive of direct care staff?

Do you consider your coworker's safety?

CHAPTER 41
INFORMATION THAT SHOULD BE GIVEN TO THE POLICE

If you the care provider are in danger or the client is in danger, call the police for assistance - Call 911 (if this service is available within your region.)

What is a dangerous or potentially dangerous situation?

Someone is threatening to harm you. If the person who is threatening you is wielding a weapon (a projectile, a knife, a gun), your life is in jeopardy. You need immediate police assistance.

Someone is threatening to harm himself/herself, has the means to do so, and is refusing to go to the hospital.

When calling the police what should you say?

- Identify yourself and state what your emergency is.
- State the address of the emergency.
- Be prepared to give the following information to the police:
- Does the person who is threatening have any weapons?
- What is the physical description of the person who is

threatening you (height, weight, clothing, hair color and length?)
- Where is the person who is threatening you right now? (Is he/she still in the facility? If so, what room is he/she in?)
- Is the person who is threatening you under the influence of drugs or alcohol?
- Does the person threatening you have a history of violence or suicide attempts?

Tips:

USE PHRASES SUCH AS "I NEED HELP", "THERE IS AN ASSAULT IN progress here", and "There is an assault with a weapon in progress here"

- Be clear and concise in your descriptions.
- If you are frightened, tell the police this.
- If you have the opportunity to run and get away from the person who is threatening you, do so.
- If, after dialing 911 or the local emergency number, you find that you do not have the opportunity to speak to the operator, don't hang up. Leave the phone off the hook; the call will be traced, and help dispatched to you.

Proactive Tip: EVERY WORKSITE SHOULD HAVE A VIOLENCE prevention program in place that includes comprehensive policies & procedures. One important aspect of a violence prevention program is that of designating a "safe place" that you would be able to readily secure yourself for your own personal protection. Ideally, this location should provide you with the ability to observe the situation, yet provide for your personal protection. Telecommunications to notify the authorities should be readily available.

AWARENESS

PERSONAL/ETHICAL DILEMMAS IN REPORTING ASSAULTIVE Incidents to Authorities

- Does the client's right to privacy supersede your right to an abuse free working environment?

- If the client is considered "not responsible" for their actions does that excuse them legally?

- Does your employer pressure you not to report incidents of this nature?

- Is your employer providing a safe working environment?

- Have you or a fellow worker been injured in a similar situation?

- Are the local police supportive of laying charges of this nature?

CHAPTER 42
STRESSORS SPECIFIC TO WORKING SHIFT WORK

Stressors include:

- chronic fatigue
- irritableness
- altered eating habits
- altered elimination patterns
- reduced staffing
- lack of administrative support
- restriction of social activities
- reduced quality of life
- reduced ability to handle everyday situations
- increased possibility of alcohol or substance abuse
- depression

Proactive Tip: You might be asking yourself "What does working night shift have to do with anything?" Some might answer "that if you worked night shift, you wouldn't ask that question!"

. . .

Working the night shift can have numerous physiological as well as psychological effects on a worker as described above. Being physically exhausted due to lack of sleep can magnify or distort your interpretation of a given situation and can affect your reasoning and response to it.

If you work in an environment that has a high potential for crisis or violence incidents there is all the more reason for you to have a plan in place.

Stereotypes of Male and Female Healthcare Workers in a Crisis

- males are not always the "defenders"
- females are not always in need of protection

CHAPTER 43
FIGHT OR FLIGHT? THAT IS THE QUESTION!

AWARENESS

Our bodies have an interesting way of rapidly readying us to handle a crisis. In a situation, that presents as a danger to us, our brain quickly reacts and prepares the body to either run from the threat or to stay and fight it. The brain works automatically.

From a *physiological* perspective, the brain sends a message to the adrenal glands located on top of the kidneys. The adrenals secrete epinephrine and norepinephrine (adrenaline/noradrenaline).

This reaction is often called the ***flight/fight response*** as it prepares the body for action. The adrenaline causes an increase in the heart rate and the blood pressure. The metabolic rate is increased, fat is mobilized which immediately increases the blood sugar level. As well, we experience increased sweating, cool skin and perhaps cold hands and feet.

We may feel nauseous or feelings of "butterflies in the stomach." Our mouth becomes dry and we may feel the urge to urinate. These symptoms are part of preparing the skeletal muscles for rapid movement away from the danger or to stay and fight.

The problem is that the brain's response is exactly the same for *fear, anxiety, and excitement*.

Compounding this reaction is how a person has handled crises in the past, their current state of mind and body, and if they have a repertoire of coping skills to be able to resolve a crisis.

While adrenaline helps us survive in a "flight or fight" situation it has negative effects in situations where this is not the case. It can interfere with our judgment and make it difficult for us to take the time to make good decisions.

It can reduce our enjoyment of our work. An increase in adrenaline can interfere with fine motor control when we are completing a physical task that may require a high degree of manual dexterity. It can influence how we view situations.

We may see situations as a threat, whereas others may view them as challenges. It sabotages the positive frame of mind that you need to perform high quality work by promoting negative thinking, damaging self-confidence, and narrowing attention. It also disrupts our focus and concentration which makes it difficult to cope with distractions. We become anxious, frustrated and quick to anger.

If we are exposed to increased levels of adrenaline over a long time, our health may start to deteriorate. As we said earlier, adrenaline is preparing your muscles for action. It is doing this by diverting resources from other areas of the body that are supposed to be keeping us healthy. We may see the problems that this causes in several ways: a change in appetite, frequent colds, back pain, digestive problems, headaches, generalized aches and pains. We may also experience feelings of intense and long-term tiredness as well as sexual disorders.

People suffering from Post-Traumatic Stress Disorder (PTSD) may be in a constant state of uneasiness/readiness. With the adrenals continuously releasing adrenaline into the system the person would be in a high state of anxiety and fear.

When they experience a crisis, over and above what they are already experiencing it puts their system into a panic. They may experience palpitations, tremulousness (shakes), diaphoresis (excess sweating), hyperventilations leading to parathesis (abnormal burning, tingling) of the lips and fingers, carpopedal spasms, diarrhea, urinary frequency, nausea, faintness, dizziness, dilation of the pupils, flushing of the skin, excessive facial and palmar sweating, shortness of breath, and tightness in the throat.

As if these unpleasant symptoms were not enough they may also experience feelings of helplessness, dread, apprehension, or impending disaster. Many also experience the feelings that sudden death, insanity, disorientation, or the urge to commit an aggressive or destructive act are imminently possible. Restlessness, a lack of self-confidence, and a difficulty in concentrating also occur.

Now let's take a look at this subject from the perspective of the objectives of this manual. We work regularly with a variety of people that may respond in an infinite number of ways to a given hazard. The three A's *(awareness, assessment, action)* come in to play here.

As a healthcare worker we need to be aware of how we respond to stress ourselves. Do we have unresolved issues from our past that would influence our reaction in a crisis?

Are we aware of the potential situations/hazards that we may face in our work setting?

Have we identified what skill development would help us in being more effective in a crisis?

Are we aware of these very same concerns in our fellow worker? If so, what are we going to do about it?

If our crisis involves another person, it is important to keep in mind that they too may be experiencing various degrees of the above-mentioned symptoms. As a care-giver you have to be aware of your own responses in a crisis situation. You need to perform a balancing act. Balancing your own emotional escalation, making it work with you, and at the same time remaining in control. Fear, pain and anxiety are powerful emotions to control.

To illustrate the influence of adrenaline in a crisis response, I recall two situations I was involved in while working in a psychiatric hospital. In the first one, we were sitting in the nursing station that looked out into a widened multipurpose area. Unbeknown to us, one of our female patients was becoming increasingly agitated.

We first became aware of her agitation when she threw a large, 36" high ashtray over the desk crashing on to the nursing station floor. When we came out from behind the desk to investigate and intervene she threw several smaller ashtrays at us. At this point she was out of control, growling, yelling and throwing chairs at the windows. We were on the fourth floor, the windows were supposed to be shatter proof, but you never know.

Our initial response was to try to verbally diffuse the patient, but this was quickly found to be ineffective when she attacked my partner. She had grabbed him about the head and was scratching his face with her fingernails. I intervened, wrestled her to the floor and together my fellow staff and I physically restrained her.

While we were restraining her on the floor, the rest of our team was preparing to escort her to the seclusion room (lock-up) and to administer PRN medication to settle her.

I had one of her hands pinned to the floor. She very rapidly maneuvered herself so she could chomp down on my left thumb. I was punctured on both sides of my thumb by her incisor teeth. I was very aware of the possibility of losing my thumb at any moment. From the position of my body and the positioning of hers on the floor, the only leverage point I had to extricate myself was to put my index finger of my right hand into her eye socket.

I cringe thinking about it as I write it but at that time it was either that or lose my thumb. I liked my thumb and would have preferred not to lose it. My thumb in her eye socket had the desired effect and she released her dental grip on my thumb.

At about this point the rest of our team was in place and intervened, escorting her under restraint to the seclusion room. Upon completion of our physical intervention I needed to do the paperwork part of the job.

While writing, the adrenaline that had been coursing through my veins energizing me suddenly stopped. My thumb was throbbing with pain. I had not even felt it up until now. I felt as though I was going to pass out at the desk and to be taken by wheelchair to a bed to lay down. I lay there for several hours before I was able to recover enough to go home. Years later I still find my thumb to be sensitive to pressure.

On another memorable occasion I was working the night shift on an admission ward in the same psychiatric hospital. As a male nurse I was a member of the Emergency Response Team (ERT) and carried a pager so that I was immediately available. This pager was on the left side of my belt.

On the right side of my belt was another pager. I was also the first responder for medical emergencies within the hospital.

On this particular night we received an admission from the local police. Two very large police officers escorted a handcuffed, inebriated person into the ward. The officers unhandcuffed the patient and left the building.

Within minutes of the officers leaving the parking lot, while I was attempting to interview him, the new admission went ballistic. He was striking out at us, out of control. We were only yards away from the switchboard operator so I yelled at her to call a "code."

As I was carrying the beeper, it goes off and I continue with the restraining process while awaiting reinforcements. While awaiting reinforcements, the patient has some kind of medical reaction, he stops breathing and I have to initiate CPR.

Once again, I yell at the switchboard to call a medical emergency code. My other beeper sounds off. As I was the designated first responder I had to throw my keys to another staff to get the crash cart. Both teams arrived at about the same time. It was slightly confusing to say the least.

The burst of adrenaline into my system allowed me to do what I needed to but it was an interesting scenario in having to change my role from that of physically intervening to one of savior. Once again when the adrenaline had finished its job, I was left feeling drained.

CHAPTER 44
CASE STUDY: PERCY

Case Study:

IN MY EARLY DAYS OF WORKING AS A NURSE IN A PSYCHIATRIC hospital, I was expected to be a member of the ERT (Emergency Response Team) by virtue of being a male. While carrying a pager, our role was to respond to an emergency anywhere within the hospital grounds.

This was a daunting task at times due to some of the outlying buildings being a good quarter mile away from the main building. When arriving upon the scene, our first order of priority was to ensure that we had the stamina remaining to deal with the situation we were responding to.

I recall one incident where I was summoned to Maple Unit, a unit for developmentally delayed adults with either major mental illnesses or severe behavior problems. Maple Unit was locked and secured with a double set of locked doors to pass through to gain entrance. Upon arrival I found five female staff secured in the nursing office. They had locked the office doors behind them.

Beyond their sanctuary, out in the common area walked Percy. When I say "walked" I refer to the fact that he was walking on his hands, with his feet up in the air, all the while shouting at nothing in particular. Percy was a well-built, muscular young man of nineteen years.

I entered the nursing station to find that there were two nurses, one nursing assistant who had been pulled from another floor to cover a sick call and two summer students. The nurses were anxiously shouting at me that I needed to do something about Percy. As I was the only ERT responder to this call, my first priority was to determine how I would solve this problem with the team that I had before me.

My initial response to having walked into the unit was "okay, Percy is walking on his hands again. How is this a problem?" The nurses outlined a story of how Percy had received a phone call from his mother and he was always agitated after speaking to her. He had been threatening to hurt someone. I enquired as to what their expectation of me was. They replied that they wanted me to give him PRN medication [antipsychotic/sedative] and "throw" him in the seclusion room.

I realized that a show of force was not going to resolve this situation as we didn't have a team that was skilled at restraining techniques. Only one of the nurses had taken ERT training. The rest, were unskilled at these type of situations and in fact, were quite fearful. I had worked with Percy in the past and felt that I had developed a rapport that would allow me to at least talk to him.

My plan was to talk to him in the common area. I had one of the nurses standing nearby with a liquid dose of his prescribed PRN ready to give to Percy. I sent one of the summer students down to the seclusion room to have it ready for us. The other summer student was assigned to escorting the nearby patients out of the common area. I was attempting to reduce the audience factor. Some of Percy's co-patients were quite experienced at encouraging him to act out. The other nurse was instructed and prepared to step in and physically intervene with the others, should that become necessary.

Upon approaching Percy, I was able to encourage him to sit down and talk with me. I started off with a supportive approach encouraging him to talk about what was bothering him. Basically, I let him vent his frustrations about his phone call to his mother and previous ones that added fuel to his rage.

After a few minutes of allowing him to vent, with no apparent escalation of his rage, I transitioned into a directive approach. I advised Percy that we were concerned about his personal safety and that his anger was scaring his fellow patients and the staff as well. I convinced Percy that if he took his PRN medication, he would feel better after doing so. I also told him that we would like him to go and lie down on the mattress in the seclusion room and have a sleep.

I further added that when he woke up he would feel better and could return to the common area. Percy accepted his PRN without incident and accompanied me to the seclusion room where he put on the security pajamas and lay down on the mattress. The seclusion door was locked as the final step and one of the summer students was assigned the role of maintaining 1-1 observation on Percy.

Upon returning to the nursing station for a debrief with the team, I let out a sigh of relief only to hear one of the nurses shout out "Well, we certainly blew that one!" I was taken aback and quickly asked her what she meant. "We should have grabbed him right away and dragged him to seclusion."

My immediate response was "When you say **We**, do you mean me? I would have been alone in doing that." "This is a win-win situation. Percy got his PRN medication… he is safely secured in a locked room… and nobody was hurt. How could we possibly have blown it?"

Her response was "He didn't learn anything from this. Now he will think that he can get his way anytime just by acting up. If we had dragged him in there [seclusion room] and spiked him, he would know who's boss!"

I spent some time with her and the others debriefing the situation. I explained that the goal of any interpersonal altercation is a nonviolent outcome. I also believe in the value of building bridges with people when they are well or settled so that when you interact with them when they are agitated, you have some previous rapport to leverage.

Analysis:

This entire situation might have been prevented if the staff on duty had been proactive in advance. This next section outlines what the on-duty staff *could* have done in advance i.e. earlier in their shift.

Assessment

Percy was not a new admit to the unit. He was known to display similar behavior at other times when receiving a phone call from his mother. A previously determined strategy/intervention could've been featured in his care plan to respond to an expected response from him. All staff should've been aware of the strategy.

Could there have been a way to reduce or mitigate Percy's, almost conditioned, response to his mother? Perhaps scheduling the phone calls in advance and providing Percy with preventative PRN medication to reduce his anxiety before the phone call may have helped.

The charge nurse could have taken stock of the human resources she had to manage difficulties that she might encounter in her shift. On this particular unit, having all females i.e. no males on shift, was a red flag.

The charge nurse could have been aware that only one of her fellow nurses had emergency response training. One staff was from another ward and was not familiar with the unit or its patients. The two summer students, not having much clinical background nor crisis intervention training were more of a liability than an asset.

During their initial shift report and shift planning session they could have created their action plan to include who would do what in possible situations.

Awareness

Violent, acting out behavior, while not the norm, was certainly not unusual on this particular unit. Management has a responsibility to ensure that all staff are prepared to perform the duties of the job. Having crisis intervention training for one's personal protection is integral to working on this unit. The staff also have a responsibility to make known to their managers that they are at risk in not having the experience and skills in dealing with crisis situations.

The charge nurse needs to be aware of the current conditions of the unit as well as those from the immediately prior shifts. The best predictor of the future can be to look at the immediate past.

Were all the staff on duty aware of Percy's past history of acting out and his care plan, assuming that this problem had been identified in it?

Did the charge nurse give consideration to the fact there were five females working and that an option might have been to request additional male staff or trade off to another ward?

This incident took place some time ago. What would be different if it were to happen today?

Many jurisdictions have Occupational Health & Safety Legislation in place that might address unsafe situations. In those areas that do, the worker may have the right to refuse to work in a dangerous situation. If so, the charge nurse should be aware of what constitutes a situation that would allow a worker to refuse to work. Sometimes there seems to be room for interpretation. What one person finds to be threatening may not be by another. Anyone taking on a charge role should be aware of what steps they must follow as per the legislation. A work refusal could add a dangerous element of its own if it prevented the team from taking emergency action to a rapidly developing clinical crisis.

Action

Having assessed the situation developing and being aware of Percy's recent behavior and his high likelihood of behaving similarly in the upcoming phone call with his mother, the ward staff would be in position to mitigate the situation by developing a plan of action.

The action plan could include such factors as:

- having one staff move the other patients out of the area that Percy was making his phone call
- speaking to Percy in advance of his phone call and perhaps offering him PRN medication to settle him
- contacting the Shift Supervisor of a potentially volatile situation developing to see if any extra staff could come to the unit for a while to help keep things settled
- Plans A, B & C should be developed. If Percy takes the PRN pre phone call and all goes well… then what? What if he doesn't take the PRN as offered and his behavior escalates? What should be done if he escalates and seclusion with an injection is the desired option? How will that be done in a timely manner?

Upon reflection of this incident I believe the nurse who had uttered "Well, we blew this one!" was coming from a position of fear. It can be easier to strike back with force to a danger than it would be to be proactive and develop a strategy to mitigate the consequences.

There is an old saying that goes "If the only tool that you have in your toolbox is a hammer, then every problem you have will be a nail." It is important to have various tools for intervention at your disposal. I was lucky that my intervention with Percy was successful. It could have gone sour just as easily.

CHAPTER 45
SECTION THREE SUMMARY

In Section Three we were introduced to the nature of crises and provided with examples of the characteristics of crisis-prone individuals via a Quick List. We then learned how to identify events that can trigger a crisis response. Identifying and expanding upon the four levels of a crisis were explored next. We also looked at specific attitudes or approaches that we can use in each of the four levels of a crisis.

Supportive and directive approaches were differentiated to take with a disturbed individual and the appropriate time to use them. We then followed with techniques to handle verbal aggression.

From there, we moved on to exploring how our body language works for or against us in resolving a crisis. Physical interventions were discussed. We then focused on the psychological reactions experienced by many individuals in crisis.

Techniques for utilizing a team approach in resolving a workplace crisis were explored.

There is always paperwork to be completed in any unusual situation. With the conversion to electronic charting and an electronic patient record, one has to wonder what the new phrase will be? "There is always the post crisis data entry to be completed... Doesn't have the same ring to it, does it?

We explored the legal aspects of documenting, post incident. Then we moved into exploring post incident debriefing techniques. Tips on contacting emergency responders i.e. police, fire & ambulance were explored.

Individuals handle a crisis differently. Do we stay or do we run? Chapter Four concluded with several case studies from my experience to illustrate the chapter's content.

In Section Four, we will explore how caregiver burnout can both add to the potential of violence in the workplace as well as be a possible result of the violent working conditions. We also look at ways to "fight the fire" of work-related burnout. I also share an example of how workplace violence created burnout in me personally and how I successfully overcame the singeing.

∾

SECTION FOUR:
CAREGIVER BURNOUT

CHAPTER 46
CAREGIVER BURNOUT

AWARENESS

Earlier in this manual we identified care-giver burnout as a potential cause of aggression directed towards the care-giver.

A precursor to burnout is the compassion fatigue stage. It is also known in the literature as post-traumatic stress disorder, or secondary traumatic stress disorder, or vicarious PTSD. It is viewed as a natural consequence and by-product of caring for, listening to, and helping those that are traumatized. One key indicator that caregiver fatigue may be present is the presence of persistent, intrusive mental pictures of traumatic situations and/or those traumatized.

Burnout may be defined as the gradual process of becoming worn out or exhausted because of excessive or improper use of self. Burnout typically occurs in hard-working, driven people who become emotionally, psychologically or physically exhausted.

Health care providers experience burnout when they fail to retain their objectivity and critical distance from clients and become over-involved in the empathic helper-client relationship. Burnout is a form of distancing from the intense interpersonal work of the therapeutic relationship. It is generally the result of over-responsibility characterized by working long hours, taking work home, and not allowing for leisure-time activities.

It is believed that burnout is a key factor in low staff morale, absenteeism, and high job turnover.

You are at risk of burnout where:

you find it difficult to say "no" to additional commitments or responsibilities

you have been under intense and sustained pressure for some time

your high standards make it difficult to delegate to assistants

you have been trying to achieve too much for too long

you have been giving too much emotional support for too long

Assessment

Signs of Burnout

The first signs of burnout are generally subtle and nonspecific. Burnout will normally occur slowly, over a long period. It may express itself physically or mentally.

Symptoms include fatigue, frequent colds, headaches, backaches, difficulty sleeping or getting up, and depression. Mentally, you may feel a lack of control over commitments, an incorrect belief that you are accomplishing less, an increase in negative thinking and a loss of a sense of purpose and energy. All these symptoms may lead to a detachment from relationships which in turn may cause further conflict and stress, adding to the problem.

Other cues involve avoidance of clients, withdrawal, speaking or joking about clients in derogatory ways, and feeling tired all the time.

If the burnout process continues without intervention, the burnout behavior will "spill over" into the worker's home life with resulting family and marital conflict. Emotions will become difficult to control, resulting in irritability, being quick to anger, and crying easily. The sense of self diminishes and the helper feels that role performance is not up to expectations.

It would seem evident that if we or a fellow worker were experiencing symptoms of burnout, then there would indeed be an increased risk of a workplace situation turning sour, resulting in violence. How can we possibly perform effectively in a crisis while our systems are being bombarded with adrenaline and burnout creeping up on us?

Think back to the three A's. We have just explored the *awareness* and *assessment* of burnout. This leads us into our *action* phase. How do we avoid burnout and how do we extinguish the flames it if it has already taken a hold on us?

CHAPTER 47
AVOIDING THE FLAMES
(AVOIDING BURNOUT)

Action

There is a lot of wisdom in the expression "you have to stop and smell the roses." I have adapted the intended sentiment a little to "all work and no play can make for a burned out Rae!"

It is probably easier for any of us to recognize the symptoms of burnout in a colleague than it is to see them within ourselves. The challenge then becomes to develop a plan of action we can apply to ourselves on a daily basis. If you are in danger of burning out or you are no longer enjoying what you do, the following actions can help douse the flames.

It seems rather simplistic but one of the secrets of avoiding burnout from work is to have fun. Who says that work can't be fun? Daily, we are surrounded by situations that are funny. A smile or a laugh can be contagious, spreading from fellow worker to client. Sharing a joke or a humorous anecdote can drastically improve the moral and the milieu of a workplace. Even a harmless practical joke can be effective in improving morale and reducing the chances of burning out.

Here is an example of a practical joke my fellow workers played on me:

I was working in a community-based mental health facility. I made the mistake of leaving my baseball cap at work, in the staff room, when I went home after my shift. Upon my return to work the next morning I was greeted by an effigy of myself sitting in our staff room.

The chest of my likeness was created from a Coleman cooler, the rest of the body from spare clothing, stuffed with newspaper. A large balloon formed my head with my beard and glasses drawn in. On top of the "balloon head" sat my baseball cap.

As a nurse my role is multi-faceted. Providing counseling to my clients in 1 to 1 sessions plays a major part of my job. I suppose I was gaining a bit of a reputation in the quality/quantity of my sessions among my fellow staff. Sitting upon the chest of my doppelganger was a sign saying "Rae's 1 to 1 machine. Please make your comments and select a response."

Sitting cradled in the arm of the "therapist" was a Tupperware container containing small slips of papers with possible selections written upon them. Upon investigation some responses were as follows: "Oh, please tell me more"; "I can feel your pain"; "What did you learn from this" all generic responses that could apply to almost any situation. My favorite response referred to Joe my fellow nurse and the creator of this scenario. "Yes Joe is a wonderful nurse. Please tell me more about Joe!"

My likeness sat in the staff room over the weekend. It was as if another person was actually sitting there and when we entered the room, it startled us many times. When one of our resident's psychiatrists visited, he was escorted back to the staff area to see the 1-1 machine. He laughed and said it could put him out of business!

The final laugh was when I retrieved my hat only to find that the baldness of the "balloon head" looked even more like my own receding hairline.

Another example involves a fellow worker, Marge. I was working the dayshift with her. Marge left her eye glasses sitting on the counter in the staff room. In the middle of each lens I attached a single white reinforcement. The kind one would use to repair a torn ring hole on a piece of notebook paper.

As we were going through shift change, Marge enters the office and puts on her glasses. She immediately recoils and takes off her glasses in a state of shock and bewilderment. Her reaction was hilarious causing another staff to spill her coffee. Marge later told us that for a moment she thought she was having a stroke and her vision had left her.

I personally find that using humor in a tense situation can be a very powerful tool in reducing increasing tensions. It is a tool that has to be wielded very cautiously though. I would not use it if I observed psychosis or paranoia and suspiciousness in the other person. I believe in "building bridges." I actively work at building an effective therapeutic relationship with my colleagues and clients during the "good times" so that it is much easier when we experience bad times.

Let's look at some more specific actions to reduce our chances of burning out.

Re-evaluate your goals and prioritize them.

Evaluate the demands placed on you and see how they fit in with your goals.

Identify your ability to comfortably meet these demands.

If you are over-involved, reduce the commitments that are excessive.

Learn stress management/stress reduction skills.

Examine other areas of your life that may be causing stress, such as family or friends. Try to solve the problems which in turn will reduce your stress.

Get the support of your friends and family in reducing your stress.

Ensure you are following a healthy lifestyle:

- Get adequate sleep and rest to maintain your energy levels

- Ensure you are eating a healthy, balanced diet — a bad diet can make you ill or feel bad

- Get adequate regular aerobic exercise

- Limit your caffeine and alcohol intake

Develop alternative activities such as a relaxing hobby to take your mind off problems.

When away from work, set limits on those people that would demand too much of your emotional energy. Become more unapproachable and less sympathetic.

When working with clients who are emotionally draining ensure you are maintaining adequate professional boundaries. Involve other colleagues in a supportive role.

Experiment with different relaxation methods. Progressive muscle relaxation, mediation, tai-chi and yoga have had good results.

Acknowledge your own humanity: remember you have a right to relaxation and a right to pleasure.

Visit a counselor/therapist who is familiar with problems related to working within healthcare.

Take some time away from work. Spend some time doing something for yourself!

RAE A. STONEHOUSE

CHAPTER 48
FIGHTING THE FIRE

AWARENESS

Nurses are burning out in increasing numbers. A 1998 workplace poll was conducted by the research firm of McIntyre & Mustel on behalf of the British Columbia Nurses Union (BCNU). The survey had some disturbing results. It showed that nurses were struggling with dramatic increases in workloads. 87%

of the nurses responded that they were overwhelmed by their workloads. They are also working understaffed continually and suffering from burnout in alarming ways. A startling 60% of the respondents reported over-exhaustion as a symptom in the past six months. From the choices of over-exhaustion, disrupted sleep disorder, headaches, work-related injuries, stomach problems, depression, personal problems, 45% reported experiencing three or more symptoms.

Perhaps even more disturbing, at a time when employers are facing a shortage of nurses, the poll shows that almost half of the membership would leave nursing and pursue another career if given the opportunity. As well, slightly more than half of those polled would not recommend nursing as a good career choice.

The province of British Columbia's nursing workforce is small in relation to the number of practicing nurses worldwide. Some would dismiss the survey as reflecting too small of a geographical sample to draw substantive conclusions. Others would say that this survey is indicative of what is happening worldwide. The study only polled Registered nurses. If we draw other healthcare workers into the formula, many with much fewer options than nurses, then we have a genuine crisis.

I view life as being about choices. Half of the BCNU nurses polled said they would leave nursing if they could. This is a decision that I have considered several times throughout my career. To stay or to go? That is the question.

I have spoken to many nurses who have struggled with the same question. Many expressed the feeling that they couldn't quit because they don't know how to do anything else. Burning out has a way of eroding your self-esteem and how you view life. I've decided to stay in nursing.

Forty-plus years of providing healthcare has shaped my personality. I am a nurse. I think like a nurse. I believe the skills I have honed over the years i.e. communication, critical thinking, problem solving etc., would serve me well in any other career path should I choose to do so but for now I will continue to use them within nursing.

PROTECT YOURSELF NOW!

Update: Since originally writing that last paragraph, I have retired from nursing as of January 2020.

ACTION

If you are experiencing burnout, you have several options available to you.

1) Continue to work in what you are doing and be miserable, gradually smoldering and burning out.

2) Quit your job without any thoughts or plans for your future welfare.

3) Attempting the specific actions described earlier to avoid burnout.

4) Increase your skills level so that you become more proficient in your job. In theory, this should help to relieve your stress level.

5) Educate yourself in other areas separate from the field of nursing. Diversifying your skills can make you more marketable and increase your job search options.

6) Becoming proactive in making your current working conditions more bearable.

Proactive Tip: I have met far too many nurses who believe it is heresy to even consider options. "Once a nurse, always a nurse!" is their cry.

My choice is to become proactive. This is not necessarily the easiest choice nor the least risky.

By educating yourself in areas such as occupational health & safety, labor law, interpersonal communication, conflict management, all the areas discussed in this book, you increase your ability to be able to improve your working conditions.

By taking a proactive approach to the problem your chances of avoiding burnout within yourself and others are greatly improved.

For some people, organizing or being part of a union, is the answer. For others it may not be. One way or another, a major part of the solution lays in networking with people who share the same beliefs and desires you do.

CHAPTER 49
CASE STUDY:

C **ase Study:**
I believe it to be inevitable, anyone who works for a sustained time in a profession that is as emotionally and physically demanding as the nursing profession, they will eventually experience compassion fatigue or burnout.

However, it might be better to view it as a possible *phase* of one's career and not reflect upon one's entire career. How a person responds to that phase is crucial though.

I reached that point in my career in 1987. I was working in a psychiatric hospital on an active admission ward. Three to four new admissions a day wasn't out of the ordinary. As the Charge Nurse we were responsible for knowing the clinical details of 40 patients at a time. Over the span of a month or so we had an increase in the amount of seriously psychotically disturbed patients who we admitted to the ward. Most of these new admissions were young males.

The first few days after admission can be very trying for the nursing staff and equally stressful for the patient. Psychosis doesn't follow a pattern that is repeated among each patient. Each experiences it differently which impacts how they relate to their personal surroundings. Their treatment needs to be individualized.

With so many disturbed individuals in a confined area as the ward was... tension ran high. Some patients were so psychotic that they required both chemical and physical restraint to help them settle. At this point in time, a device called a Total Body Blanket Restraint was in vogue. It required a team of staff to physically restrain a patient and wrap them in a mesh blanket containing about 10 or so straps that tied the person to their bed.

It was of questionable value in that it created a high risk to the patient should they struggle and possibly choke themselves. Others, realizing that struggling was futile, would give up fighting the restraint, relax and let the medication work on them. One to one staffing while a patient was restrained this way was instituted after a few untoward incidents.

Another form of restraint was the Seclusion Room. A seclusion room was in essence a 12 foot by 10 foot room, with the walls made of concrete cinder block. The sole furnishings of the room, a single mattress with a "safe" nightgown included. The nightgown was of a quilted style, very thick and heavy. It was supposed to be fairly indestructible. A heavy steel frame and a 2 and a half inch thick solid wood door ensured that the patient was secured safely inside. In theory! A large plastic bubble was installed in the door to allow staff to insert their head in to observe the secured patient in all positions in the room.

As a male nursing staff I was expected to participate in all physical restraining measures when I was on duty.

During this month or so that I refer to, the total body restraint and the seclusion room were in use around the clock. We had to escort several of our patients under restraint via elevator to use the seclusion room on another floor. We would then have to stay on that ward to provide observation for their safety and security.

PROTECT YOURSELF NOW!

We admitted one middle-aged fellow to the ward that required immediate restraint and seclusion in the locked seclusion room. He had recently served time in prison and had been considered "difficult" while incarcerated. Whether his subsequent actions while in seclusion were a sign of severe psychosis or severely abnormal behavior was undeterminable.

This next sentence or so comes with a caution if you the reader has a weak stomach. While secured in the seclusion room he apparently ripped open his anus with his fingernail and covered almost every square inch of the seclusion room walls with blood and feces.

In all my years of nursing this is definitely what I would consider the grossest situation I have encountered. Now imagine having to sit on a bar stool, in front of the seclusion room door, with your head inserted into the bubble so to observe the patient, for hours on end. All the while he continued to decorate the room in gore, throwing and smearing it on the bubble. He was pounding on the bubble, screaming and swearing continuously. Now imagine that the supposedly secure and solid wood door that he had been kicking upon gives way freeing him from his forced confinement.

The next few moments were utter chaos.

After working for a month or so in this high anxiety climate I was experiencing the accumulated effects of the anxiety. It culminated at 0600 hours one morning for me while working the night shift, over seemingly a minor incident with a young male patient. My recollection of the incident is somewhat unclear at this point in time but it was over control of the remote control for the television. He was being challenging, at least that is how I viewed it at the time and I "lost it" as the saying goes. I verbally responded to his opposition quite forcefully.

Upon finishing my shift, I was quite upset with how the shift had progressed and ended. Not so much that the young fellow had been difficult but how I had personally lost control and responded to him. It was not in my nature to respond that way.

After considerable thought on the matter I correlated my increasing anxiety and distress to the working conditions on the ward to my out of character response. Continuing in this matter was not acceptable to me. I went to my doctor and requested time off work. I was subsequently away from work for seven weeks on sick leave. "Stress leave" as some might call it.

Being off on stress leave was quite a revelation to me. My physician was of little help. "Just take time off from work and forget about the place" was his response. Here I worked in a psychiatric hospital and yet there was no one that I felt that I could talk to about my stress. There were a few that I could have spoken to. However, having worked alongside of them and knowing them personally, I had little faith in their ability to help me. I certainly didn't want to reveal any vulnerabilities that would come back to haunt me when I returned to work. This was at a point in time where employee assistance programs hadn't been developed yet.

My stress was compounded by the fact that much of my social network was based around friendships that I had developed with my work colleagues. If I spent time with my friends, I would have to hear about everything that was continuing to go on in the workplace. If I didn't associate with them, I became isolated.

After much soul searching, I came to the conclusion that the working conditions were not going to change and the only leverage point available to me was to change the way I looked at the situation. I started spending time at the library and researching workplace stress and how it affected people. Upon return to work I made the decision to apply for a transfer to a less demanding ward. I also made the decision that my future did not lay in continuing to work for the next 30 years in this facility or environment. I set out a plan to relocate to another part of the country. Within a year of being on stress leave, I was close to 3000 miles away from the workplace stress.

Were my new location and working conditions stress free? Certainly not, however I was able to sleep at night without the thought that I was going to be killed or seriously injured at work.

Was picking up and moving across the country an impulsive act or one of avoidance? No I don't believe so. I didn't like the way that my future would likely unfold if I remained there.

Were there other options for employment closer to home? Likely, however we were persuaded and encouraged by the milder climate and potential opportunities at the new location.

There was quite a bit of strategizing and logistical challenges to overcome to achieve this major geographical move, including selling a house at one end, building a new one at the other end. My wife was also a nurse and we moved without having jobs waiting for us. It was stressful in moving away from family but there were also unexpected benefits of doing so. Distance from relatives tends to reduce friction.

At the point of writing this section, I have gone on to work another 30 years in my chosen field of nursing. What if I had given up and left the profession when I experienced those extremely stressful working conditions? Many of my colleagues did leave our profession. I recall one leaving to open up a gas station, another to open a convenience store. Many developed alcohol and drug dependency issues. A few suicided.

When we are in the middle of an intense situation, it is easy to lose focus on what matters in life. It is easy to believe that we are the only person that has ever gone through a stressful situation as we are experiencing. It is easy to believe that there is nobody out there to help us through the situation. There is! You have to reach out and ask for help though. Your friends and family are not mind readers. They may see you suffering but not know why. They may want to help but don't know what to do. Your solution to a problem may not be on as grand a scale as mine was but I believe that there are solutions to every problem. Sometimes it takes a while away from the problem to allow the solutions to present themselves.

∽

CHAPTER 50
SECTION FOUR SUMMARY:

In Section Four we explored caregiver burnout at some length. Could you relate personally to some factors and effects discussed? If not in yourself, perhaps in a friend or colleague? We also explored a personal story of mine that provided the impetus to write this manual.

In Section Five we explore critical incidents in our worksites and how they can affect us at different levels. We also explore post-traumatic stress disorder and we will probably wonder if we all carry some of that with us.

∼

SECTION FIVE:
CRITICAL INCIDENTS

CHAPTER 51
CRITICAL INCIDENTS

Awareness

People who respond to or witness emergencies are exposed to highly stressful events. Sometimes, an event is so traumatic or overwhelming, that those responding or witnessing may experience significant stress reactions. These events are known as **psychological traumas** or if they occur in the workplace **critical**

incidents.

Critical incidents may produce a wide range of stress symptoms, which can appear immediately at the scene, a few hours later or within a few days of the event. Stress symptoms usually occur in four different categories: Cognitive (thinking), Physical (body), Emotional (feelings), and Behavioral (actions). The more symptoms experienced, the more powerful the stress reaction has been. The longer the symptoms last, the more potential there is for permanent harm. The following is only a sample of some of the changes you might experience after a critical incident.

Cognitive:

poor concentration

time distortion

difficulty making decisions

flashbacks (images keep returning)

poor attention span

disorientation

memory problems

slowed problem solving

difficulties with calculations

Emotional:

depression

agitation

guilt

uncertainty

loss of emotional control

panic

anxiety/fear

shock

feeling lost/overwhelmed

numbness

grief

anger

emotional shutdown

PHYSICAL:

nausea

dizziness and/or fainting

muscle tremors

muscle soreness and fatigue

headaches

hyperventilation

stomach upset

sweating

chest pain

breathing difficulties

elevated blood pressure

. . .

BEHAVIORAL:

excessive silence

pacing

withdrawal from contact

moody and short with people

changes in eating habits

resentful

sleep disturbance

irritable

changes in work habits

unusual behaviors

AWARENESS

Critical Incident Debriefing

Critical incident debriefing is a process of resolving the individual's immediate psychological crisis and restoring them to at least the level of functioning that existed before the crisis period.

This process can be enacted via peer support programs or trained Critical Incident Stress personnel (traumatologists.) In the case of the peer debriefer, they are acting in a "crisis intervention" role — not a counseling role: connecting with the worker, helping them get grounded, educating them about CIS (Critical Incident Stress) and CIS resources and directing them to professional support when necessary.

Critical incident debriefing can be quickly summed up as:

"Walk it out, Talk it out... **Let it go**"

An in depth exploration of critical incident debriefing is beyond the intent or scope of this book.

CHAPTER 52
STRESS SURVIVAL SUGGESTIONS
TALK IT OUT

Action

When someone experiences a significant stress from a critical incident, the following steps may help to reduce the stress until the incident is over or until a trained Critical Incident Stress Debriefer Team (CISD) is accessed:

LIMIT EXPOSURE to sights, sounds and odors

PROVIDE AN IMMEDIATE REST of at least 25 minutes

PROVIDE FLUIDS — non-alcoholic and non-caffeinated

PROVIDE FOOD low in salt, sugar and fat

ALLOW THE PERSON TO TALK about the experience

DO NOT RUSH THE PERSON to return to work

PROTECT THE PERSON from bystanders and the media

REASSURE THE PERSON that the stress experienced is normal; most people recover very well from stress

SHOW APPRECIATION for the person's work

DO NOTHING TO EMBARRASS THE PERSON

HELP THE PERSON MAKE DECISIONS

REMOVE THE PERSON FROM THE SCENE if necessary, but always as a last resort

TAKE THE PERSON TO A HOSPITAL if chest pain or respiratory distress is present

CHAPTER 53
SELF-CARE POST TRAUMA

Traumatic stress tests our coping mechanisms to the limit. Because of the impact on your psychological system, a variety of coping mechanisms appear -- some healthy, some not so healthy. Keep the following in mind:

1. **DO NOT USE ALCOHOL OR OTHER DRUGS TO COPE.** Drugs, in particular alcohol, are powerful symptom suppressers - *they numb the pain BUT they don't solve the problem...* Talk it out --work through the problem -- don't medicate *it*.

2. **DO NOT ISOLATE YOURSELF.** Many people react to psychological trauma by keeping it inside. Often the trauma may seem so great that life seems meaningless. By withdrawing, you keep yourself in the dark causing the incident to become larger than life. Though you may need some time alone, eventually get talking.

3. **EAT WELL AND MAINTAIN A PHYSICAL OUTLET.** Diet is an important factor in reducing the negative effects of stress. Even though you may not feel hungry, eat something and make sure it's healthy food. Exercise is critical to cleansing the body of the negative consequences of stress. Get some good exercise within 24

hours of the incident. Do not stop with that. Keep up regular activity, whether it's a tennis game, a run, or a swift walk.

4. **ASSESS YOUR WORK SITUATION CAREFULLY.** If the incident happened at work, and if you are very traumatized by an incident, it may be necessary to take time off from work. Working while being emotionally vulnerable puts you at risk for an acute stress reaction. On the other hand, you may be someone who finds that being back on the job is just what is required. Assess your situation carefully. If you feel ready for action, return to work. If you feel vulnerable, request time off but seek professional help.

5. **WATCH YOUR FIXATION ON THE INCIDENT -- ALLOW TIME TO HEAL.** Sometimes we become *obsessed* with the tragedy. We can't get it out of our minds. Shocked by what has happened, we feel a need to regain meaning or a sense of fair play in life. Whether we are looking for simple or complex answers, the solution does not come immediately. Allow time to pass. Only over time will the real meaning of what has happened become apparent and assist you in choosing a direction for life.

6. **EXPECT THE INCIDENT TO BOTHER YOU.** Take comfort in knowing the incident will not bother you forever. Though you will never actually totally forget the incident, remembering it does not have to cause extreme emotional distress. Your goal should not be to totally forget the incident. Rather, it should be to heal. You know you are healed when you are able to think of or talk about the incident without profound emotion.

7. **LEARN ABOUT TRAUMATIC STRESS.** You need facts about what you are going through. Get a book on traumatic stress. Through reading you will feel less abnormal and learn a way to assist in your recovery. One good self-help book is I Can't Get Over It, by A. Matakis.

. . .

8. TAKE TIME FOR FUN. YOU MUST TAKE CARE OF YOURSELF-- that includes doing what you enjoy. Take time for leisure activities. Active ones are particularly helpful.

9. GET HELP IF NECESSARY. IF YOU FIND THE INCIDENT IS staying with you longer than it should, seek individual counselling. Talking with a trained professional can prevent long-term distress.

CHAPTER 54
ADVICE TO MATES & FRIENDS

If a friend, colleague, or mate has experienced a traumatic event, your behavior may help in their recovery. Here are some suggestions:

1. **LEARN ABOUT TRAUMATIC STRESS.** Learn about traumatic stress so you can begin to understand what they are experiencing.

2. **ENCOURAGE THEM TO TALK.** Encourage them to talk about how they are feeling about the incident, but do not be overly demanding. They may feel that others do not want to hear about their feelings or that you expect them to be able to "handle it." You need to challenge these beliefs by indicating your willingness to listen.

3. **DON'T BE INTRUSIVE.** Ask, "How are you doing?" or "How are you feeling?" If they want to talk they will, if not, they won't. However, by asking, you have sent the message that a "listening ear" is available. If they never want to talk, at some point ask them why. They may be talking to others and your knowing this will help alleviate your stress. If they are not, encourage them to do so.

4. LET THEIR EMOTIONS FLOW. Do not be afraid of the expression of extreme emotion. Many of us have not experienced profound grief and anguish. Seeing someone cry uncontrollably can be a little distressing. A traumatized individual needs to let emotions out. Your supportive presence is often all that is needed. Simply be with them and let them release their emotions. Afterwards, take them for a walk to shed the chemistry of stress.

5. REFLECT YOUR FEELINGS, BUT DON'T TELL THEM HOW THEY'RE FEELING. Share your feelings about the situation. Do not say, "I know how you are feeling," because you don't. You may have gone through a similar experience, but not through their experience or as seen through their eyes. You can say things like "I found it tough when I went through a similar experience," or "I can imagine this must hurt really bad," or "I feel so sorry for what has happened."

6. NO FALSE PROMISES. Do not give false promises such as "Everything will be OK." No one knows the future. See your role simply as a support person, not as a Mr/s. Fix-It. If you do not know what to say, say nothing. In most cases what people need is someone to "hear them out," not necessarily make it better. Say, "It's OK to feel the way you do." Affirm that this has been a horrible tragedy, and it makes sense that it will be painful, confusing, or whatever. This helps particularly if you are a peer -- an equal. It feels good to have your coworkers legitimize your feelings.

7. DO NOT MINIMIZE THEIR SITUATION. DO NOT TRY to explain away anything. At this stage your explanation is not needed -- emotional release is. Your explanation may be experienced as a discount of their feelings, not as a supportive comment.

8. MAKE SURE THEY ARE HEALED. ENCOURAGE A subsequent debriefing or counseling session if their distress persists. Guidelines are difficult to provide, however, each week should bring progress. Indications of progress include hearing comments such as "Yeah, I'm feeling better today," seeing less stress and strain on the individual or seeing the individual become more themselves. For most incidents, if you do not see some shift in one week, encourage them to get extra help.

9. **TAKE CARE OF YOU.** Take care of yourself. You are probably being affected by the incident through their reactions. Make sure there is someone with whom you can talk things out. If they are your family member, it is often helpful to attend one counseling session together.

∼

CHAPTER 55
POST-TRAUMATIC STRESS DISORDER

AWARENESS

Definition:
Post-Traumatic Stress Disorder (PTSD) is a natural emotional reaction to a deeply shocking and disturbing experience. It is a normal reaction to an abnormal situation.

Post-Traumatic Stress Disorder is defined in DSM-IV-TR, the fourth edition of the American Psychiatric Association's Diagnostic and

Statistical Manual. For a doctor or medical professional to be able to make a diagnosis, the condition must be defined in DSM-IV or its international equivalent, the World Health Organization's ICD-10.

IN THE PREVIOUS VERSION OF DSM (DSM-III) A CRITERION OF PTSD was for the sufferer to have faced a life-threatening event; this criterion was present because a) it was thought that PTSD could not be a result of "normal" events such as bereavement, business failure, interpersonal conflict, marital disharmony, working for the emergency services, etc., and b) most of the research on PTSD had been undertaken with people who had suffered a threat to life (e.g. combat veterans, especially from Vietnam, victims of accident, disaster, and acts of violence). In DSM-IV this requirement has been eased; it is now recognized that PTSD can result from many types of shocking experience.

NOTE: THE CURRENT EDITION IS DSM-V.

DSM-IV diagnostic criteria

The diagnostic criteria for PTSD are defined in DSM-IV as follows:

A. The person experiences a traumatic event in which both of the following were present:

1. the person experienced or witnessed or was confronted with an event or events that involved actual or threatened death or serious injury, or a threat to the physical integrity of self or others;

2. the person's response involved intense fear, helplessness, or horror.

B. The traumatic event is persistently re-experienced in any of the following ways:

recurrent and intrusive distressing recollections of the event, including images, thoughts or perceptions;

- recurrent distressing dreams of the event;
- acting or feeling as if the traumatic event were recurring (e.g. reliving the
- experience, illusions, hallucinations, and dissociative flashback episodes, including those on wakening or when intoxicated);
- intense psychological distress at exposure to internal or external cues that symbolize or resemble an aspect of the traumatic event;
- physiological reactivity on exposure to internal or external cues that symbolize or resemble an aspect of the traumatic event.

C. Persistent avoidance of stimuli associated with the trauma and numbing of general responsiveness (not present before the trauma) as indicated by at least three of:

1. efforts to avoid thoughts, feelings or conversations associated with the trauma;
2. efforts to avoid activities, places or people that arouse recollections of this trauma;
3. inability to recall an important aspect of the trauma;
4. markedly diminished interest or participation in significant activities;
5. feeling of detachment or estrangement from others;
6. restricted range of affect (e.g. unable to have loving feelings);
7. sense of a foreshortened future (e.g. does not expect to have a career, marriage, children or a normal life span).

D. Persistent symptoms of increased arousal (not present before the trauma) as indicated by at least two of the following:

1. difficulty falling or staying asleep;
2. irritability or outbursts of anger;
3. difficulty concentrating;
4. hypervigilance;
5. exaggerated startle response.

E. THE SYMPTOMS ON CRITERIA B, C AND D LAST FOR MORE than one month.

F. THE DISTURBANCE CAUSES CLINICALLY SIGNIFICANT distress or impairment in social, occupational or other important areas of functioning.

THE FOCUS OF PTSD IS A SINGLE LIFE-THREATENING EVENT OR threat to integrity. However, the symptoms of traumatic stress also arise from an accumulation of small incidents rather than one major incident. Examples include:

- repeated exposure to horrific scenes at accidents or fires, such as those endured by members of the emergency services (e.g. bodies mutilated in car crashes, or horribly burnt or disfigured by fire, or dismembered or disemboweled in airplane disasters, etc.) repeated involvement in dealing with serious crime, e.g. where violence has been used and especially where children are hurt breaking news of bereavement caused by accident or violence, especially if children are involved

- repeated violations such as in verbal abuse, physical abuse and sexual abuse
- regular intrusion and violation, both physical and psychological, as in bullying, stalking, harassment, domestic violence, etc.

WHERE THE SYMPTOMS ARE THE RESULT OF A SERIES OF EVENTS, THE term Prolonged Duress Stress Disorder (PDSD) may be more appropriate. Whilst PDSD is not yet an official diagnosis in DSM-IV or ICD-10, it is often used in preference to other terms such as "rolling PTSD" and "cumulative stress".

AWARENESS

Causes of PTSD

PTSD RESULTING FROM ACCIDENT, DISASTER, WAR, TORTURE, kidnap, etc. has been extensively studied and literature is available elsewhere. Within the healthcare field, and previously within this manual, we have identified critical incident stress as a potential cause of PTSD. We also explored burnout symptoms that could be indicative of Prolonged Duress Stress Disorder (PDSD) or PTSD.

. . .

Why are we focusing on PTSD?

Does any aspect of the description of PTSD apply to you? Hopefully not! However, it may to a coworker or colleague. What one person experiences as an extremely stressful event, may not be to another. How we process the situation is also unique to the individual. As healthcare providers we often deal with stressful situations. If we don't successfully resolve those situations at the time, we can carry our scars with us. Experiencing another stressful incident, whether similar to the original or completely different, can trigger a PTSD response in an individual.

Awareness that this is happening is crucial to your dealing with the situation at hand and in the longer run, maintaining a successful career in healthcare. I have known more than a few fellow workers who have chosen to leave our profession due to critical incidents. Some, are crippled with fear if a situation arises that is similar... in their minds, to a critical incident they were involved in.

There are others who display PTSD symptoms with the mere mention of an individual's name, if that person has wronged them in the past. In our next two chapters we discuss Horizontal Violence and Bullying in the Workplace, two categories that can create personal trauma for many people.

∼

CHAPTER 56
SECTION FIVE SUMMARY:

I n Section Five, we explored how critical incidents in our workplaces can have a detrimental effect to our well-being and our ability to function with the activities of our daily living when we aren't even at work. We discussed ways to support a coworker that has experienced an event that distresses them.

IN SECTION SIX WE EXPLORE THE TOPIC OF HORIZONTAL VIOLENCE and learn how it is more common that we probably thought. We explore techniques and protocols that will help in your worksite.

WE EXPLORE AN EXAMPLE OF A WORKPLACE CONDUCT AGREEMENT that you can adapt to your worksite. We are then presented with some guidelines on how to handle conflicts constructively.

SECTION SIX:
HORIZONTAL VIOLENCE

CHAPTER 57
HORIZONTAL VIOLENCE

AWARENESS

Definition:
Horizontal Violence is harmful behavior, via attitudes, actions, words, and other behaviors that is directed towards us by another colleague. Horizontal violence controls, humiliates, denigrates or injures the dignity of another. Horizontal violence indicates a lack of mutual respect and value for the worth of the individual and denies another's fundamental human rights.

PROTECT YOURSELF NOW!

. . .

SOME EXAMPLES OF HORIZONTAL VIOLENCE MAY BE:

NAME-CALLING, THREATENING, INTIMIDATING, BELITTLING

Gossiping, talking behind the back

Sarcastic remarks

Ignoring or minimizing another's concerns

Slurs based on race, ethnicity, religion, gender, or sexual-orientation

Pushing, shoving, throwing objects

Physical threats or intimidation

Inappropriate or unwelcome physical contact

Sexual harassment

Limiting the right to free speech and to have and state an opinion

Behaviors which seek to control or dominate another

Elitist attitudes based on education, specialization, or clinical area of practice

Nurse manager practices such as chronic understaffing; belittling the concerns of nurses; and disregard for the safety, physical or mental health of nurse employees

COPYRIGHT © JULY 1998, 1999 BY BARBARA MATHEWS BLANTON, Carrie Lybecker, and Nicole Marie Spring. Reprinted with permission.

THROUGHOUT THE FORTY PLUS YEARS OF MY NURSING CAREER I HAVE often heard fellow workers saying "You know, this would be a great job if it weren't for the patients... the other staff... management..." We work in a business that requires extensive communication skills, conflict management and interpersonal relationship skills.

Yet, if we had to determine the root cause of most of our problems, I am willing to bet that they lie within deficits of these three skills.

Within our work settings we interact with a group of people, working toward a common goal but often coming from very different backgrounds. Each of us is an amalgamation of our past experiences, our values, our beliefs and the environments that we have lived in. Research has shown that 80% or more of healthcare workers come from dysfunctional backgrounds. Perhaps a young girl is thrust into the position of having to care for her family when her mother becomes ill.

Another young woman becomes the head of the family when her alcoholic parents abdicate responsibility in raising her siblings. After achieving a certain sense of accomplishment they decide that they are suited to the care giving profession. More than likely, they have developed the skills of empathy and nurturing that are needed to care for another in a time of need.

On the downside, they may also bring to the workplace their dysfunctional coping skills, communication techniques and ways of interacting with their peers. Combine that with others with similar problems and we have a recipe for chaos, or at the very least, conflict.

I suppose that part of being dysfunctional is not being aware that you are. When I look back at my early years in nursing, with the acquired wisdom of many years of experience, I realize that I would warrant the classification of having been dysfunctional. I had more than my share of interpersonal conflict, actually more than several people's shares. I can recall thinking that it would be great to be a hermit, living alone and never having to deal with others.

I BELIEVE IT WOULD BE HELPFUL TO LOOK AT THE TERM "dysfunctional" in a different way. As nurses, I think we are quick to label any behavior that we disapprove of as being dysfunctional. We use our personal values, biases and prejudices as a filter in our labeling. In essence, if a person handles a given situation in a way that is ineffective or destructive to themselves or others, then they would be considered having been dysfunctional. This so-called dysfunction may merely be that the individual has a deficit of knowledge in certain areas. Areas that readily come to mind are interpersonal communication skills, assertiveness, effective coping skills, self-confidence and self-esteem.

IN THE EARLY STAGES OF WRITING THIS MANUAL I WAS UNAWARE OF the concept of horizontal violence as described above. Oh sure I knew that it existed, it was all around me. As I look at some examples of horizontal violence, I would have to answer "guilty as charged." It is very easy to justify one's own behavior when everyone else around you is doing the same.

I COULD VERY EASILY WRITE AN ENTIRE BOOK ON EXAMPLES OF horizontal violence that I have witnessed and if the truth be known, participated in. I am sure that any reader that has worked in healthcare for a while can do the same. It serves no purpose to dwell on the past, however, we can learn valuable lessons from our mistakes and our shortcomings.

FOR ME PERSONALLY, MY RESCUE FROM THE PITS OF DYSFUNCTION, occurred as a result of considerable personal growth on my part. I researched and added skills to my repertoire. Diverse areas such as assertiveness training, the basics of interpersonal communication, conflict management and resolution, leadership skills, self-confidence building, public speaking, effective coping skills, critical thinking and problem solving to name a few. Increasing one's skills are of limited value if you don't put them into practice. This has been a long process of trial and error. Learning from what went wrong or didn't work and honing the skills that were effective.

Recent research has determined that in many cases healthcare workers have taken on the characteristics of oppressed victims. Many of those oppressed have taken on the characteristics of the oppressors. There is a common belief within the nursing profession that "nurses eat their young." This is in reference to the way that some experienced nurses treat their newer less experienced colleagues. I am sure that you have seen most of what has been identified as horizontal violence behavior within your fellow workers.

Following the Three A's as used throughout this book (*awareness, assessment, action*) we continue to delve into increasing your awareness of horizontal violence within your work setting. I urge you to reflect upon situations, conflicts that you have had in the past and think about what you could have done differently. I say "you" because that is where the change for the better is going to occur. You can change yourself but not the other person. Looking at a particular situation, determine the skills or knowledge that if you had possessed at that time would have made a difference to the outcome of the situation.

PROTECT YOURSELF NOW!

ACTION

OUR THIRD A IS THAT OF ***ACTION***. WHAT ARE WE GOING TO DO about it? I am hoping that everyone reading this is of the agreement that horizontal violence is unacceptable. We are in positions to make changes for the better. As with many changes there is an element of risk involved on our part. It requires us to become more vocal in expressing our disapproval of horizontal violence that we witness. It means holding ourselves out as role-models and not participating in it. It means sharing and educating others in what is acceptable behavior and what is not.

TAKING ACTION BEGINS WITHIN OURSELVES. BE SENSITIVE ABOUT your behavior to others. As our workload increases and the pressures of our jobs intensify, it is easy to deliberately or unintentionally say or do something that could produce a strong negative reaction in others. This could bring out a similar response in the other person, leading to a stronger negative reaction.

SOME HELPFUL SUGGESTIONS AT THIS JUNCTURE WOULD BE:

- to be aware of how you are feeling about a particular situation or person

- to treat everyone from subordinates to supervisors with dignity and respect
- to never speak to anyone in a condescending, demeaning manner and to be open to feedback and constructive criticism.

Remember that it's not what you do, but how you do it that can be the difference between successfully resolving an issue and creating an incident.

I encourage you to improve your skill repertoire in the areas that I mentioned earlier. This will vastly improve your self-confidence and your ability to serve as a change-agent. A specific strategy may be to start a dialogue on the subject at work. Copy out the statement of horizontal violence and use it as a topic of discussion at a staff meeting. Encourage your supervisor to incorporate the philosophy into your policies and procedures manual. Here is an example of a workplace behavior contract that you may want to consider adapting to suit your needs. At the very least it could serve as a tool to open discussion on ways to improve the workplace.

CHAPTER 58
EXAMPLE OF A WORKPLACE CONDUCT AGREEMENT

PREAMBLE:
Nurse, Mental Health Worker, Maintenance Worker and Life Skills Worker are all bound by these guidelines. As coworkers committed to creating a better working environment, we are all equals, and as such, can feel comfortable enforcing these workplace rules when deviations occur.

GUIDELINES

1. **Take ownership for expressing your own needs:**

IMMEDIATELY COME FORWARD AND EXPRESS YOUR FEELINGS WHEN uncomfortable one on one.

MAKE EVERY EFFORT TO RESOLVE DIFFERENCES, CLARIFY POTENTIAL misunderstandings when they occur, or before you go home.

. . .

PROGRESSIVE STEPS IN CONFLICT RESOLUTION:

A) When a coworker says or does something that bothers you, discuss it ASAP with them rather than dwelling on it or sharing it with others not involved.

B) IF UNABLE TO RESOLVE YOUR DIFFERENCES, NOTIFY THE TEAM Leader of your concerns, providing as much objective detail as possible.

C) FOLLOWING A DISCUSSION WITH EACH OF THE INVOLVED PARTIES, a meeting between the Team Leader and the affected individuals will be arranged if the matter is not satisfactorily resolved.

D) IF RESOLUTION FAILS TO OCCUR FOLLOWING THESE STEPS, THE matter will be referred to any applicable individuals for further discussion.

BE OK WITH ASKING FOR HELP, BE OK TO SAY YOU DON'T AGREE with something. It's your right!

DO NOT ASSUME! IF YOU ARE UNSURE OF SOMETHING SAID OR DONE, it is your responsibility to obtain clarification.

2. BE AWARE OF THE IMPACT YOUR COMMENTS HAVE — CHECK it out.

SOMETHING HUMOROUS OR INNOCENT TO YOU MAY BE OFFENSIVE TO others. Use your empathetic skills.

. . .

A) IF YOU THINK SOMETHING YOU WANT TO SAY WILL unnecessarily violate or upset the other party, err on the side of caution, and keep it to yourself.

B) DO NOT SWEAR, RAISE YOUR VOICE OR ATTEMPT TO INTIMIDATE when discussing issues with others. It is your responsibility as a staff member to role model effective interpersonal skills, regardless of how an issue affects you personally.

C) BEFORE YOU COMMENT, CHECK YOUR PROXIMITY TO RESIDENTS. If they hear, how might they interpret it?

D) IF YOUR MOOD IS AFFECTING HOW YOU INTERACT WITH OTHERS, say so.

E) IN A SMALL FACILITY LIKE OURS, AN INDIVIDUAL'S ACTIONS AND comments can easily affect the morale of everyone else. Despite the varied personalities and philosophies, we are committed towards improving our working relationships and how we are viewed by our peers in the Health Region.

3. ACCEPT INDIVIDUAL'S VIEWS AND ISSUES WITH RESPECT.

A) You have the right to disagree with someone, staff or resident, but you do not have the right to judge, persecute or ridicule someone because of his/her view. Respect is a two-way street, and must be earned, rather than expected.

B) WHEN YOU HAVE REACHED AN IMPASSE DUE TO A DISCREPANCY IN opinion, agree to disagree, and move on.

. . .

C) Abuse of authority, regardless of the issue, is _ABUSE_!

D) Staff members in a supervisory role have a responsibility to maintain facility standards on his/her shift.

E) Direction to subordinate staff must be given appropriately. Every staff member is part of the team, regardless of his/her role.

Note: It is important to interject here that if you create and adopt a conduct contract for your worksite, you need to review it often. A document that hangs on the wall collecting dust, serves no purpose. It is meant to be a tool. Use it as one. As situations occur at work that have been addressed in the contract, draw attention to the particular clause or statement. The contract is meant to be a living document and should be used as a tool that offers practical solutions to workplace situations.

CHAPTER 59
SEVEN GUIDELINES FOR HANDLING CONFLICTS CONSTRUCTIVELY

Action

There is a helpful article by Thomas Jordan entitled 'Seven Guidelines for Handling Conflicts Constructively' available at https://www.mediate.com/articles/jordan2.cfm

1. **Ask yourself what it is you don't know yet.** Keep in mind you don't know what story is foremost in other people's minds.

Each individual has his or her own story about what is important and why. Insight into these different stories can make a great difference for how you and other people handle the conflict. Take on conflict situations with an intention to understand more about what is going on. Ask open-ended questions, questions that help you to understand the background of the conflict better. People's images of what is significant in specific situations are important causes to how they behave. These images can change. Remember also to remain open to learning new things about yourself and how other people perceive you. Maybe other parties feel that you have contributed more to the problems than you are aware of.

2. **Separate problem and person.** Formulate the conflict issues as shared problems that you need to solve cooperatively. Abstain from blaming and voicing negative opinions about others. State clearly what you feel and want and invite your counterpart to help finding solutions. Opinions and emotions should be expressed in ways that facilitate the process of achieving satisfying outcomes. Keep in mind that there is always some kind of positive intention behind people's actions, even if unskillfully expressed.

3. **Be clear, straightforward and concrete in your communication.** State clearly what you have seen, heard and experienced that influenced your views in the matter at hand. Tell the other person what is important to you, why you find it important, what you feel and what you hope for. Express you own emotions and frustrated needs in clear and concrete words. Ask for the counterpart's feelings and needs in a way that conveys that you care about them.

4. **Maintain the contact with your counterpart.** Breaking off the contact with the counterpart in a conflict often leads to a rapid conflict escalation. Do what you can to keep the communi-

cation going. Work to improve your relationship even if there are conflict issues that seem impossible to resolve. Offer to do something small that meets one of your counterpart's wishes and suggest small things your counterpart can do to meet your own needs and wishes. Even if marginal, such acts can strengthen the hope that it will be possible to change the nature of the relationship in a positive direction.

5. LOOK FOR THE NEEDS AND INTERESTS THAT LIE BEHIND concrete standpoints. Bargaining about standpoints often leads to stalemates or unsatisfying solutions. Inquire into what needs and interests would be satisfied by certain concrete demands and explore if there are alternative and mutually acceptable ways of satisfying those needs and interests. Regard blaming, accusations and negative opinions as unskillful ways of expressing emotions. Show understanding for the feelings of the counterpart without letting yourself be provoked by the attacks you are the target for. Inquire into what is really important and significant for yourself and keep those values and needs in mind during the course of the conflict.

6. MAKE IT EASY FOR YOUR COUNTERPART TO BE CONSTRUCTIVE. Avoid triggering the defensiveness of your counterpart by blaming, accusing, criticizing and diagnosing. Extend appreciation and respect for the counterpart where you can do so sincerely. Show you counterpart that you care about the issues and needs that are important to him or her. Take responsibility for your own

contributions to the conflict events.

7. DEVELOP YOUR ABILITY TO LOOK AT THE CONFLICT FROM THE outside. Review the conflict history in its entirety. Notice what kinds of actions influence the tensions of the conflict in positive and

negative directions. Take care to develop your awareness of how you can influence the further course of events in the conflict in a constructive direction. Test your own image of what is going on by talking with impartial persons. Assume responsibility for what happens. Take on problems you see as early as possible, before they have a chance to develop into major conflict issues.

THOMAS JORDAN

Thomas.Jordan@av.gu.se

COMPILED FROM:

FISHER, R. & URY, W. (1981) Getting to yes. Negotiating agreement without giving in, Boston: Houghton Mifflin Co. GLASL, F. (1999) Confronting conflict. A first-aid kit for handling conflict, Stroud: Hawthorne Press.

ROSENBERG, M. (1999) Nonviolent Communication: A Language of Compassion, PuddleDancer Press.

STEINWEG, R. (1999) Arbeitsklima und Konfliktpotential, Erfahrungen aus oberösterreichischen Betrieben, WISO Dokumente, Heft 45, Linz:

Institut für Sozial- und Wirtschaftswissenschaften.

STONE, D., PATTON, B. & HEEN, S. (1999) Difficult conversations. How to discuss what matters most, New York: Penguin Books.

--

THOMAS JORDAN, PH. D. TEL.WORK. (+46) (0)31 7735437

Department of Work Science Tel. home (+49) (0)2196 82179

PROTECT YOURSELF NOW!

Gothenburg university Thomas.Jordan@av.gu.se

Box 700 Thomas.JordanGU@t-online.de

SE-405 30 Goteborg, Sweden

From the author: "You are free to use this is if you find it helpful (even post it on your own website) as long as you don't modify the text without my permission"

CHAPTER 60
SECTION SIX REVIEW

In this section we defined horizontal violence and some causes of it. We also looked at action steps that we take to reduce the damage caused by horizontal violence and prevent it in our workplace. We explored a workplace conduct contract example and we looked at some guidelines for handling conflicts constructively.

IN SECTION SEVEN WE WILL IDENTIFY WHAT BULLYING IS AND WHY some people bully. We will explore how to spot an employer that bullies. We will learn techniques to regain control of our lives and the decisions that we make. We will also learn practical steps that we can use to take the power away from a bully and look at a couple of case scenarios that illustrate a bully in action.

SECTION SEVEN:
BULLYING IN THE WORKPLACE

CHAPTER 61
BULLYING IN THE WORKPLACE

AWARENESS

Closely related to horizontal violence is another dysfunctional workplace behavior, bullying. According to the late Tim Field creator of Bully Online, bullying differs from harassment and discrimination in that the focus is rarely based on gender, race, or disability. The focus is often on competence, or rather the alleged lack of competence of the bullied person. In reality, the target of bullying is often competent and popular, and the bully is aggressively projecting their own social, interpersonal and professional inadequacy onto their target. The purpose of projection is to avoid facing up to that inadequacy and doing something about it, and to distract and divert attention away from the bully's inadequacies, shortcomings and failings.

WHAT IS BULLYING? BULLYING IS PERSISTENT UNWELCOME behavior, mostly using unwarranted or invalid criticism, nitpicking, fault-finding, also exclusion, isolation, being singled out and treated differently, being shouted at, humiliated, excessive monitoring, having verbal and written warnings imposed, and much more. In the workplace, bullying usually focuses on distorted or fabricated allegations of underperformance.

WHY DO PEOPLE BULLY? THE PURPOSE OF BULLYING IS TO HIDE inadequacy. Bullying has nothing to do with managing etc. ... good managers manage, bad managers bully. Management is managing; bullying is not managing. Therefore, anyone who chooses to bully is admitting their inadequacy, and the extent to which a person bullies is a measure of their inadequacy. Bullies project their inadequacy on to others:

a) to avoid facing up to their inadequacy and doing something about it;

b) to avoid accepting responsibility for their behavior and the effect it has on others, and mainly,

c) to divert attention away from their inadequacy - in an insecure or badly-managed workplace, this is how inadequate, incompetent and aggressive employees keep their jobs.

BULLYING IS AN INEFFICIENT WAY OF WORKING, RESULTING IN disenchantment, demoralization, demotivation, disaffection, and alienation. Bullies run dysfunctional and inefficient organizations; staff turnover and sickness absence are high, whilst morale, productivity and profitability are low. Prosperity is illusory and such organizations are a bad long-term investment. Projection and denial are hallmarks of the serial bully.

Bullying is present behind all forms of harassment, discrimination, prejudice, abuse, persecution, conflict and violence. When the bullying has a focus (e.g. race or gender) it comes out as racial prejudice or harassment, or sexual discrimination and harassment, and so on.

∼

CHAPTER 62
HOW TO SPOT A BULLYING EMPLOYER

You may be dazzled by corporate visions, mission statements, or by impressive badges on glossy paper, and whilst in some cases these may be deserved, some quality and people awards can be used by unscrupulous employers to hide what's really going on. The best guide to what it's really like to work for an employer is to obtain the following information covering at least the last twelve months. A good employer will be happy to divulge this information. (Apart from stress breakdowns, some employers, especially the larger ones, may have a small number of these for genuine or unrelated reasons):

- rate of staff turnover
- amount of sick leave
- number of stress breakdowns
- number of deaths in service
- number of ill-health retirements
- number of early retirements
- number of uses of disciplinary procedures
- number of grievances initiated
- number of suspensions

- number of dismissals
- number of uses of private security firms to snoop on employees
- number of times the employer is involved in industrial tribunals or legal action against employees

CHAPTER 63
PEOPLE WHO ARE BULLIED FIND THAT THEY ARE:

People who are bullied find that they are:

- constantly criticized - explanations and proof of achievement are ridiculed, overruled, dismissed or ignored
- forever subject to nit-picking and trivial fault-finding (the triviality is the giveaway)
- undermined, especially in front of others; false concerns are raised, or doubts are expressed over a person's performance or standard of work - however, the doubts lack substantive and quantifiable evidence, for they are only the bully's unreliable opinion
- overruled, ignored, sidelined, marginalized, ostracized
- isolated and excluded from what's happening (this makes people more vulnerable and easier to control and subjugate)
- singled out and treated differently (for example everyone else can have long lunch breaks, but if they are one minute late it's a disciplinary offence)
- belittled, degraded, demeaned, ridiculed, patronized
- threatened, shouted at and humiliated, especially in front of others

- taunted and teased where the intention is to embarrass and humiliate
- set unrealistic goals and deadlines which are unachievable or which are changed without notice or reason or whenever they get near achieving them
- denied information or knowledge necessary for undertaking work and achieving objectives
- denied support by their manager and thus find themselves working in a management vacuum either overloaded with work (this keeps people busy [with no time to tackle bullying] and makes it harder to achieve targets) or have all their work taken away (which is sometimes replaced with inappropriate menial jobs, e.g. photocopying, filing, making coffee)
- have their responsibility increased but their authority removed
- have their work plagiarized, stolen and copied - the bully then presents their target's work (e.g. to senior management) as their own
- are given the silent treatment: the bully refuses to communicate and avoids eye contact; often instructions are received only via email, memos
- subject to excessive monitoring, supervision, micro-management, recording, snooping, etc.
- the subject of written complaints by other members of staff (most of whom have been coerced into fabricating allegations - the complaints are trivial, often bizarre ["He looked at me in a funny way"] and often bear striking similarity to each other, suggesting a common origin)
- find requests for leave have unacceptable and unnecessary conditions attached, sometimes overturning previous approval, especially if the person has taken action to address bullying in the meantime
- denied annual leave, sickness leave, or especially compassionate leave
- when on leave, are harassed by calls at home or on holiday, often at unsocial hours
- receive unpleasant or threatening calls or are harassed with

intimidating memos, notes or e-mails with no verbal communication, immediately prior to weekends and holidays (e.g. 4 pm Friday or Christmas Eve - often these are hand-delivered)
- do not have a clear job description, or have one that is exceedingly long or vague; the bully often deliberately makes the person's role unclear
- are invited to "informal" meetings which turn out to be disciplinary hearings
- are denied representation at meetings, often under threat of further disciplinary action; sometimes the bully abuses their position of power to exclude any representative who is competent to deal with bullying.
- encouraged to feel guilty, and to believe they're always the one at fault
- subjected to unwarranted and unjustified verbal or written warnings
- facing unjustified disciplinary action on trivial or specious or false charges
- facing dismissal on fabricated charges or flimsy excuses, often using a trivial incident from months or years previously
- coerced into reluctant resignation, enforced redundancy i.e. layoff, early or ill-health retirement

CHAPTER 64
AS AN INDIVIDUAL, WHAT CAN I DO ABOUT IT?

Assessment

PROTECT YOURSELF NOW!

Bullying is hard to prove, as it takes place behind closed doors with no witnesses and no evidence (in the traditional sense at least). When called to account, the bully uses charm and their Jekyll and Hyde nature to lie convincingly. Bullies are clever, but you can be clever too.

HERE'S HOW:

STEP 1: REGAIN CONTROL

- Recognize what is happening to you as bullying - it is the bully who has the problem which he or she is projecting on to you.

- Criticisms and allegations, which are ostensibly about you or your performance and which sometimes contain a grain (but only a grain) of truth, are not about you or your performance. Do not be fooled by that grain of truth into believing the criticisms and allegations have any validity - they do not. The purpose of criticism is control; it has nothing to do with performance enhancement.

- Criticisms and allegations are a projection of the bully's own weaknesses, shortcomings, failings and incompetence; every criticism or allegation is an admission by the bully of their misdeeds and wrongdoing, something they have said or done - or failed to do.

- You may be encouraged to feel shame, embarrassment, guilt and fear - this is a normal reaction, but misplaced and inappropriate. This is how all abusers, including child sex abusers, control and silence their victims.

- You cannot handle bullying by yourself - bullies use deception, amoral behavior and abuse of power. Get help. There is no shame or failure in this - the bully is devious, deceptive, evasive and manipulative - and cheats. Often, the bully is behaving in the manner of a sociopath.

Action

Step 3: Take action

- Keep a log (journal, diary) of everything – it's not each incident that counts, it's the number, regularity and especially the pattern that reveal bullying. With most forms of mystery, deception, etc. it's the patterns that are important. The bully can explain individual incidents but cannot explain away the pattern. It's the pattern which reveals intent.

- Keep your diary in a safe place, not at work where others can steal it; keep it at home and keep photocopies of important documents in a separate location (not at work); in several cases the bully has rifled the desk drawers of their target, stolen the diary and then used it as "evidence" of misconduct.

- Keep copies of all letters, memos, e-mails, etc. Get and keep everything in writing otherwise the bully will deny everything later.

- Carry a notepad and pen with you and record everything that the bully says and does. Also make a note of every interaction with personnel, management, and anyone else connected with the bullying. Expect to be accused of "misconduct" and a few other things when you do this.

- Record everything in writing; when criticisms or allegations are made, write and ask the bully to substantiate their criticisms and allegations in writing by providing substantive and quantifiable evidence. When the bully doesn't reply or fails to supply substantive and quantifiable evidence, write again pointing out you've asked for justification and the bully has chosen not to reply or has failed to justify their claim. On the third occasion point out, in writing, that making allegations and refusing to substantiate them in writing or failing to provide substantive and quantifiable evidence is a form of harassment. The bully's criticisms and allegations, which are usually founded on distortion, blame and fabrication, are an opinion or fabrication for the purpose of control.

- Denial is everywhere. The person who asserts their right not to be bullied is often blowing the whistle on another's incompetence (which the bullying is intended to hide). Expect the bully to deny everything, expect the bully's superiors to deny and disbelieve everything, expect personnel/human resources to disbelieve you and deny the bullying, for they will already have been deceived by the bully into joining in with the bully and getting rid of you.

- The serial bully likes to play people off against each other so try to reunite yourself with your employer against the bully. Point out firmly but politely to your HR people that the serial bully is encouraging the employer and employee and to engage in destructive conflict in which there are no winners, only losers. The bully gains gratification from manipulating and watching others destroy each other. If the bully realizes they've been rumbled they will move on leaving the employer to incur all the vicarious liability for their behavior. The bully has done this before and will do it again.

- Build yourself a support network. Bullies separate and isolate their targets, sometimes going as far as to cause division within the target's family. The bully is likely to be manipulating your work colleagues into distancing themselves from you, either by sweet-talking them with charm, or by playing on their vulnerabilities whilst raising doubts about their job security.

- See your doctor - bullying causes prolonged negative stress which results in psychiatric injury.

- Psychiatric injury has nothing to do with mental illness, despite what others (including some mental health professionals) may say or infer. If stress is diagnosed, make sure it includes the cause, e.g. stress caused by conditions in the workplace. If depression is diagnosed, make sure it is recorded as reactive depression. Remember that stress is not the employee's inability to cope with excessive workload but a consequence of the employer's failure to provide a safe system of work

- Take the matter up with your line management - beware though, most bullies are the line manager and are supported by their line manager, etc. Often, the bullying is hierarchical and comes from the top.

- Obtain a copy of your employer's bullying and harassment policy. You might wish to do this discreetly (e.g. through a third party) if you're not yet ready to challenge the bully.

- Contact occupational health - bullying causes prolonged negative stress which results in injury to health and if it continues may culminate in psychiatric injury.

- You are unlikely to be the only person contact your OH department - and you may not be the first to name the bully.

- Reassure and educate your partner/family that your symptoms are a psychiatric injury and will get better. Encourage those around you to read up on bullying and PTSD (Post Traumatic Stress Disorder).

- Inform your employer that your psychiatric injury (and the ill health of others) is due to bullying by another member of staff and that this employee's behavior is a danger to the health & safety of employees; highlight the high staff turnover in that individual's department and the corresponding amount of sickness absence / stress breakdowns / early and ill-health retirement / attempted or actual suicides / deaths in service.

- Follow the grievance procedure, but beware that such procedures may be biased in favor of the manager, as well as being inappropriate for dealing with bullying.

- Understand the profile of the serial bully and emphasize the Jekyll and Hyde nature and compulsive lying. The bully will already have deceived personnel and his/her superiors. If you go to an employment tribunal later, the tribunal will look to see if you've followed all the options open to you (regardless of whether they work or not).

- If the bully prevents you from being accompanied to grievance and disciplinary meetings, check your rights under your country's law.

- If the bully is making unwarranted criticisms in public or on your record, you may feel it appropriate to ask your solicitor to write a letter to the bully pointing out that he or she is subject to the laws of slander, libel and defamation of character.

- If your employer refuses to get involved, or backs the bully in his/her attempt to get rid of you, you might consider asking your solicitor to write to someone in authority (with legal responsibility) outlining the way your manager has treated you, stating that your rights in law will be vigorously defended against the unacceptable behavior of one of their employees whose actions will be monitored as a consequence of his or her declared intentions. This turns the spotlight on the bully rather than on the target. If your employer is unwilling to address the bullying - perhaps because the bullying is hiding incompetence which is endemic in the organization - expect fireworks.

- Consider leaving - regard it as a positive decision in the face of overwhelming odds which are not of your choosing, not of you making, and over which you have no control. Serial bullies are obsessive and compulsive in their behavior; once they start on their target, they won't let go until that person is destroyed.

- For most people, the top priority is to be financially stable. What's more important - job or health? You may need to make the decision to move on and find an employer who values you and your skills. Refuse to allow your health to be destroyed and your career wrecked by an idiot.

- If you are forced into leaving, make it clear to your employer in writing that this is due to bullying. Get professional advice before signing anything.

- Do your utmost to obtain an agreed reference. Without one you may not be able to get another job, especially in the professions. Most employers require a reference from your previous employer and the bully never misses the opportunity to sabotage your career.

- The Number One mistake people make is to not recognize the serial bully as a sociopath. Naivety is the greatest enemy - most people can't or won't believe that the person they're tackling is a sociopath and consequently expect the bully to recognize their wrongdoing and make amends. Sociopaths cannot and will not - but they will ruthlessly exploit other people's naivety to ensure their own survival. Never underestimate the serial bully's deviousness, ruthlessness, cunning, and ability to deceive.

PHRASES YOU MIGHT FIND USEFUL:

"BY THE WAY S/HE CHOOSES TO BEHAVE, S/HE PREVENTS MYSELF AND others from fulfilling our duties."

"BY THE WAY S/HE CHOOSES TO BEHAVE, S/HE BRINGS HER/HIMSELF, the staff, the department and the employer into disrepute."

"THE PURPOSE OF BULLYING IS TO HIDE INADEQUACY; BULLYING IS A breach of the implied term of mutual trust and confidence."

"YOUR CRITICISMS AND ALLEGATIONS LACK SUBSTANTIVE AND quantifiable evidence."

IF YOU ARE FIGHTING A CASE OF BULLYING AGAINST A SERIAL bully and the employer chooses to not respond positively, remember the Achilles heels:

- Bullying is an obsessive-compulsive behavior and therefore repetitive; it's often a lifetime behavior. It is most likely the serial bully has a history of this behavior which a little investigation will reveal.

- The serial bully displays an arrogance and fully expects to get away with their behavior.
- Serial bullying is highly predictable; this site describes the profile of the serial bully.
- The serial bully is usually a compulsive liar with a Jekyll and

Hyde nature - therefore their word cannot be trusted. Highlight this at every opportunity.

- When dealing with the serial bully, concentrate on the patterns of incidents rather than the incidents themselves (which are often trivial when taken out of context). The bully can always explain away individual incidents, but s/he cannot explain the pattern. When discussing any single incident, refer repeatedly to the pattern of which this incident is part.

- Bullies are adept at creating conflict between those who would otherwise pool negative information; make it clear to your employer that the bully is working his or her own self-interest and gains gratification from encouraging the employer and employee to engage in destructive conflict. Remind your employer that the bully is deliberately and willfully causing the employer to incur vicarious liability for their behavior.

- The purpose of bullying is to hide inadequacy, and people who bully to hide their inadequacy are often incompetent; the worse the bullying, the greater and more widespread the incompetence. Abusive employers will often pay large out-of-court settlements to keep that incompetence secret.

- If all else fails, and legal action proves impossible, remember Klingon wisdom: bortaS bIr jablu'DI'reH QaQqu' nay' which translates as Revenge is a dish best served cold: give media interviews, write articles, contribute to research, or write a book ... use those qualities of competence, popularity, integrity and courage of which the bully was jealous and envious.

THE ABOVE DISCUSSION ON BULLYING WAS ADAPTED FROM information posted on Bully Online circa 1996. **Tim Field** the owner of the site had granted permission to disseminate and use the material. Sadly, Tim has passed on. Supporters of his cause have gone on to create the Tim Field Foundation and Bully Online is available at https://bullyonline.org

SOMETHING TO KEEP IN MIND ABOUT WHAT WE HAVE JUST READ IS that it refers to a person who has some form of power over you i.e. a boss or supervisor. It could very well be a coworker who is the bully or at least displays bully-like behavior. Remember, that one of the causes identified for bullying is an inadequate personality. A coworker could easily target you if they are the bullying type and utilize that type of behavior in the workplace.

CHAPTER 65
LEGAL ACTION

Intervention Process for Horizontal Violence & Bullying
Review Incident - Gain Control - Find Help - Plan for Action - Document - Confront - Formal Written Complaint - Legal Action

INCIDENT

Gain Control Recognize that the aggressor is at fault — not you. Take the time you need to acknowledge the impact of the incident and the emotions it triggers for you. Consider taking action immediately during the incident of soon after. Know that only 25% of targets and witnesses feel able to confront the bully during the incident, 75% do not. Confronting may involve disengaging from the bully.

Find Help from your union if you are a member of one, colleagues and your employer. Read your workplace policy on harassment or violence to understand your options.

Make an Action Plan Gather the support you feel you need, rather than proceeding alone. Seek advice from others with similar experiences, talk to your union steward (if you have one), your manager (assuming they are not the bully!) or counselor, and take advantage of employee assistance programs.

Document Use the 4Ws --- who, what, when & where and explain the context of the situation. Keep a detailed log of all incidents with names of witnesses. If your health is affected by these events, see your healthcare provider.

Confront the aggressor. Make it clear that the behavior is offensive and must stop. Speak from the first person point of view using the word "I" and describe the specific behavior and how it made you feel. You do not have to do this alone, gather any support you feel need before, during and after the intervention.

Make a **formal written complaint**. Follow the employer's respectful workplace complaint policy (if they have one)

Take Legal Action It may be appropriate if the situation remains unresolved to consider seeking expert legal advice.

Thus far our explanation of bullying has been fairly generalized to cover all vocations or work environments. It certainly exists in healthcare. I would expect that we have all experienced it at some time in our careers but perhaps weren't aware of what was happening to us. Or conversely, if we were aware, we felt powerless to do anything about it.

Field, having been bullied himself at work, puts it into perspective and calls it for what it is ... workplace violence. He outlines methods of recognizing a workplace bully and strategies to neutralize them. His books are a must read for anyone who is currently experiencing bullying behavior or advocates on behalf of others.

CHAPTER 66
PERSONAL EXPERIENCE WITH A SERIAL BULLY

I would like to share with you a personal story of my experience with a serial bully in the workplace. It has provided me the impetus to finish and publish this book that you are currently reading. It has been more than two decades since the incident. It can take a while to recover from the symptoms of PTSD. Some don't. I was one of the lucky ones.

In 1999 I was writing this book with the focus on violence in the workplace. I had included a section on bullying but was blind-sided when I became a victim myself.

To set the scene, I was an active participant in an online web forum entitled Nurse Advocate. Its mandate was to raise awareness and provide resources to reduce workplace violence. I regularly provided feedback and/or suggestions to support people, healthcare providers, that had experienced violence in the workplace. Common themes of discussion were the isolation the person felt, the lack of support from their fellow staff or their managers, the insinuation that they had brought the violence on to themselves and the range of negative emotions that resulted.

I was working in a psychiatric unit in a small community as a staff nurse in a casual capacity. Casual, meaning that I was on call for all of my shifts. After three years of casual I was successful in obtaining a full-time, albeit temporary position to replace another nurse who was off on extended sick leave. Three days into this new position, things changed rapidly.

I was well aware I was working in a dysfunctional workplace. There were staff who wouldn't work with others due to a disagreement ten years earlier. Some would change their schedule so as not to have to work with certain individuals. The dysfunction started at the top with the manager and trickled downward. There was a sense of oppression quite evident where the staff were afraid to voice their opinions in a public forum. The manager was overt in her attempt to split staff, one against the other. She also had her group of confidants that kept her apprised of events. She was reported to have gone through staff waste paper baskets after work hours looking for evidence to use against individual staff.

In a united front, the ward staff organized an off-duty meeting with union stewards in attendance to develop initiatives to deal with this bullying manager. Different initiatives were forwarded. Some ideas were a little more militant than others. I tend to be a logical, pragmatic thinker and offered that those suggestions were inappropriate. I tried to provide some levity to the situation by making a joke. "We are not dealing with a logical person here. The only logical thing is to pass a hat, take a collection and put a hit on her." Yes, dear reader, I can hear you cringing at this point. I would do anything as the saying goes to take that utterance back. Life doesn't work that way though. At the time, after a few laughs, it went unnoticed... until the next day.

I received a summons to attend a disciplinary hearing to account for my issuing death threats. I was in a state of shock and really wasn't aware of what they were talking about. Fortunately, one of the benefits of being in the temporary position was that I was a member of our local union which provided me representation. I brought my steward with me to my surprise disciplinary meeting.

At this meeting I learned that one of my fellow nurses, a confident of the leader being discussed, had recorded the meeting. She had contacted the manager that evening and advised them that there was an assassination plot to wipe out all senior management and that Rae's wife was a trained marksman and was going to carry out the hit. As incredulous as it seems, I was actually presented with this information. For the record, my wife, also a nurse, has never touched a firearm and abhors hunting of animals of any sort.

During the hearing, I apologized profusely for making a "black humor" joke that was taken the wrong way and was sorry for any problems that it had caused. This fueled the bully's righteous indignation and I was terminated on the spot. My union immediately intervened and filed a wrongful dismissal grievance.

Upon returning home, I contacted the RCMP (Royal Canadian Mounted Police) to find out if there was a bench warrant out for my arrest. This is a common practice to deal with situations such as this from a Human Resources perspective. I spoke with the investigating officer who thanked me for contacting him. He advised me "I was called into do an investigation at your workplace as I was asked to do. I advised your managers that it was a joke taken the wrong way, for the wrong reasons. Son, you work in a dysfunctional place. If I were you, I would get out of there as soon as you can."

Thanks to the efforts of my union, within two weeks, I was working in a facility a few blocks away from the original setting, with the same clientele. I was in a different job and it took three grievances and a year for the process to resolve itself.

I'm sure you can appreciate the stress and anxiety this created for me and my family. It was compounded by information I was hearing from my former work colleagues of how others had said they were affected by this event. It is interesting to see how people can turn against you when it serves their purpose.

A year later, this situation was resolved with a win/win outcome. I secured a new job in a better environment. I received a cash payout to rectify my losses and they got an experienced nurse at the new setting. I had an "invisible" notation on my personnel file that should I utter the same suggestion again, the notation would become "visible." This was to be on file for 18 months. That is an example of how a bully can save face.

What about the bullying manager? In an interesting twist of the story, a year or so later, a meeting of some 65 professionals met to discuss how she had impacted each of them negatively. Physicians, social workers, nurses, psychologists... all shared their stories of how she had hurt them personally.

Three unions went to the CEO of the organization and she was immediately "unhired" . She wasn't actually terminated. It allowed senior management to save face. An era had come to an end. But was she ever held accountable? We don't know. Since then she has had problems keeping jobs. A bullying manager is not acceptable.

I don't want to leave you with the idea that I was an innocent victim in this situation. I was stupid in several ways and I take full responsibility for my actions. I was stupid in that I underestimated the lengths a bully will go to maintain control. I was stupid in that I provided the bully ammo, so to speak, to take action against me to remove me as a threat.

It had occurred to me sometime after the event that I had gone on public record shortly before my termination in opposing an initiative that she was promoting. I was also stupid for saying what I did, even though it was meant as a joke at the time. I later heard in a conversation that the manager had actually targeted me two years earlier and had made the comment publicly that she would get me sooner or later. Bullies will always get even.

So what did I learn in this situation?

I learned first-hand the effects of post-traumatic stress disorder (PTSD). I experienced intrusive thoughts for close to a year. Just thinking about the manager would cause me to be distressed. I had many sleepless nights. It caused me to be hypervigilant in performing my job. What was coming next? It caused me to mistrust my former coworkers and my new ones. I became reluctant to talk to anyone as you never know if what you say will come back to haunt you as when it is taken out of context.

I know of fellow workers that if you were to mention this manager's name, they would start to display PTSD symptoms. That is the effect that a bully can have on you if you let them.

There was a turning point for me though. As we were approaching the one-year anniversary and an arbitration hearing to finally resolve this matter, it occurred to me that they could take my job away from me but they couldn't take my dignity. I had lots of other options available to me should I lose my nursing license. That isn't what a bully wants. They want you to lose hope. They want to take your dignity. That is how they maintain control and feel good about themselves. This realization strengthened me and allowed me to be an active participant in the resolution process.

I also found the whole situation to be quite embarrassing. Working in healthcare for so many years, I don't embarrass very easily, but this situation did. Here I was writing this book on workplace violence, having done a significant amount of research on the subject and I go and commit it myself. It just shows me how insidious workplace violence is. We aren't always aware of its presence. And we aren't aware of how our actions can be used against us. As the police officer said... "by the wrong people, for the wrong reasons."

Since then, I have made it my mission in life to challenge anyone that is using a similar type of dark humor. It is inappropriate and certainly dangerous. You don't know how it will be interpreted. I have shared my story with many people in the hope they won't have to experience what I did.

As I sit here at the keyboard writing this chapter I'm finding it interesting, if not somewhat depressing, reflecting on the number of other incidents throughout my life where I have come up against bullies. There always seems to be another around the corner! Perhaps the reflecting upon the bullies that I have encountered in my life has caused me to delay finishing the writing of this manual.

As a child I was easily intimidated. At six years of age a bully at my bus stop threw my pet cat under the wheels of the school bus. She had followed me several times before to the stop and then returned home on her own after I had left in the bus. In the days following, I viewed the blood stain of my pet on the pavement as I awaited my bus. Sixty years later, I still remember the incident vividly. The following year, at a different school, I was forced into paying protection money to a "tomboy" of a girl, so that she wouldn't beat me up. In an odd twist of fate I understand that she eventually became a kindergarten teacher. Those poor children!

Children that are bullies often become bullies as adults. My father was a bully and used intimidation and force to rule his family. I have no way of knowing if he was a bully when he was young but I know for a fact that his mother, my grandmother, definitely was. I was hit regularly whenever one of my siblings had gotten into trouble. "You're the oldest. It's your job to keep them out of trouble!" I remember him being a very angry man.

Using the adage of "if the only tool in your tool box is a hammer, then every problem is a nail", then we as children were his nails.

One of the observations I have had about some bullies is that when you do confront them on their behavior, they can be truly surprised that they are seen that way by others. Then their feelings are hurt and they take it personally. I haven't found mention of it in my review of the literature, but I believe there is a class of bully I would call the "situational bully."

The situational bully is displaying many of the bully-like behaviors that are consistent to what we have read above but their motive is different. At a conscious level I don't know if they are aware of how they are relating to others, or perhaps it is a conditioned response.

We all respond differently to different personality types, often based on our past experiences with similar types of personalities. We often repeat our ways of interacting with types of people who we have previously had problems with, in similar ways with others that bear a resemblance, at least in our minds, to those original ones.

This is dysfunctional. Bullying is still bullying and it isn't acceptable. The point I really want to make here is that while it is usually fairly easy to recognize bullying in other people and if you are being bullied, you will know. However, will you recognize it in yourself? It is easy to fall into a pattern of bullying if you are in a situation you don't have the skills to effectively handle it.

This section is intended to raise your awareness and leave you with a sense of hope. We don't have to put up with bullies anymore.

Note: My personal comments throughout this book reflect a 40-year nursing career. As of January 2020, I retired from nursing.

I went on to work another 20 years in the position and the location I was awarded as part of my grievance settlement. It had a happy ending with me becoming a valued employee and nurse however, it was a tortuous journey to get to that point.

It took me several years to recover from the bullying incident. I became a union steward myself for the purpose of ensuring others wouldn't go through the same struggles I did. I became an anti-bullying advocate and challenged bullying in my workplace.

I developed influence within the facility by taking a leadership role in our Occupational Health & Safety program as well as becoming a mentor for my support staff.

I had considered going back to work on a casual basis however, Covid-19 prevented me from doing so.

As I reflect upon 40 years of nursing, I'm aware I was fear-based throughout my career. I've encountered many bullies over the years, almost all were in leadership positions.

My wife, also a nurse shares a similar philosophy and that is "waiting for the other shoe to drop."

As nurses we held an inordinate amount of responsibility. Our organizations tended to play the blame game. I'm happy to say these organizations bought into the concept of being learning organizations.

As learning organizations, they started to look at causes and effects of incidents strategically, rather than the age-old reaction to finding blame and punishing someone.

CHAPTER 67
CASE STUDY: CALLEY'S STORY

Calley provides an enlightening story of the pressures she experienced in starting to work in a dysfunctional workplace. Names have been changed to protect the guilty.

Imagine how it would be to finally find meaningful employment as a Care Aide after a long and tedious job search only to find that your new worksite is toxic. And the toxicity was aimed at you... the newcomer. Or so it seems, from your perspective.

From the first days of her orientation to the new job, Calley noticed her fellow staff weren't all that friendly towards her. It wasn't obvious at first but Calley could sense that they were treating her differently.

Conversations would stop when she walked into the office. When her coworkers were going for a "coffee run" she wouldn't be asked if she was interested. Her contributions in shift report or staff meetings were dismissed by certain staff. "When you've been here long enough, you'll see things differently." "What do you know, you're new here!"

Yet at the same time, everybody else seemed to get along fine.

There always seemed to be a party at somebody's home. Calley wasn't invited. Some of her coworkers would switch their shifts so that they could work with each other or to work with a certain nurse when they were in charge. Calley found she seemed to be taking most of her coffee breaks alone. Her fellow staff would have other matters to tend to when their coffee break was due.

Calley relates "I expected some challenges when starting a new job... being the new kid on the block, but this seemed over the top."

Several months into working at her new job, Calley sensed that some residents seemed to act differently when nurse Flo, was on shift. Some of them seemed to be more sedated than what would be expected. Others, seemed timid or perhaps fearful in the presence of Flo. When Flo was on duty, many residents received sedation. Flo liked the unit to be calm. It didn't matter what time of day it was, Flo liked her residents to be quiet.

On several occasions Calley had observed Flo shouting and berating residents for their behaviour. Calley related that she felt intimidated by Flo so didn't confront her directly but mentioned her observations to a few of her fellow care aides. She was met with hostility and further shunning. The "old" staff seemed to protect this nurse and condone the behavior.

Calley reported her concerns to the Team Leader who in turn, dismissed those concerns. They spoke in support of Flo. At about this time Calley was spending a considerable amount of her off duty time thinking about her working conditions. She found her sleep was restless at times with intrusive dreams of work. Perhaps it was time to start looking for another job?

On a couple of occasions Calley observed Flo shouting at residents from the medication room, down the hall, to come and get their medications. This seemed to be acceptable by her fellow staff and nobody seemed concerned when she voiced her opinions that this wasn't a respectful way to treat residents.

The final straw, so to speak, came one day when Calley observed Flo shaking a resident. The resident was watching TV and Flo approached the resident grabbing them by both shoulders and shaking. "When I tell you that medications are ready I expect you to get your ass over there and get them! Do you hear me? Are you deaf? You better do as you are told or you will be sorry!"

Calley shared this story with her fellow Care Aides and found no support. She reported it to her Team Leader and experienced a similar response. It was only when the resident themselves approached the Team Leader to complain, was action taken. The local Licensing Department was contacted and Flo was suspended pending investigation.

Was this the end of the story? Not according to Calley... it was only the beginning! Flo started a phone campaign to smear Calley and make life miserable for her. Each of the staff were phoned and advised that "Calley was a rat." "Don't turn your back on her, she will stab you!"

This flowed back to the worksite where her fellow staff who had been avoidant and dismissive of her now became openly hostile. Flo took on a victim role and created a story where she was the wrongfully treated hero of the saga. Guess who was the bad guy?

Calley's time at work became absolute misery. Fellow staff would call her "Bitch" to her face and behind her back. Similar sentiments were scrawled on pieces of paper and stuck to the front of her locker. One nurse was openly hostile towards her. "Bitch. I hope you're happy, you've ruined the life of a good nurse. You don't deserve to work here. No wonder nobody likes you!" This was repeated several days in a row when Calley was scheduled to work with this nurse. Calley was losing sleep at night and started to phone in sick when she had to work with these staff.

As part of the investigation Calley was asked to document her observations of the abusive nurse, which she did reluctantly. No other staff submitted support for her. It was Calley's word against the nurse's. The resident's testimony was not given much weight.

Flo was eventually returned to duty with a sanction on her personnel record. She maximized her victim role and relished the power that it gave her in the worksite. Calley left the worksite due to the continuing pressure. She eventually returned after a couple years. Many of the staff who had worked there at the time had moved on, but not Flo. She continued to make sure that every staff that worked there was aware that "Calley was a rat!" Every interaction she had with Calley from then on, was openly hostile.

If you were to ask Calley today whether she would do it again, she would respond "No way! It was absolute Hell what they put me through. Nobody should be treated that way."

Flo's behavior eventually caught up with her and incompetence in nursing practice lead to a fellow nurse taking actions with the nursing licensing board. Flo was suspended from practice and chose to retire.

Analysis:

ASSESSMENT

If we take a closer look at this story what can we take away or learn from Calley's experiences?

Starting off with **Assessment**, what do we know about this worksite?

1. There seems to be an "old boys" network in place or a clique. Newcomers were not welcomed into it.

2. There was a shroud of silence where workers didn't talk or even acknowledge the untoward actions of others.
3. Interpersonal hostility towards new staff was the norm rather than the exception.
4. Certain staff had more "power" over others than what was part of their job description.
5. The residents were not treated respectfully at times.
6. The Team Leader and presumably administration condoned dysfunctional behavior by one of its nurses or at least ignored dealing with it.
7. Reporting inappropriate actions by fellow staff resulted in you being labeled as a rat.
8. Passive aggressive behavior was rampant, e.g. open messages left on lockers.
9. Aggressive behavior was tolerated.
10. Lack of cohesiveness and inclusiveness with new and existing staff i.e. us vs. them mentality, with the "us" being the existing staff.

Awareness

Moving on to **Awareness**, it would seem obvious to most of us that this was a dysfunctional worksite. More pointedly, there is strong evidence of interpersonal aggression, hostility, bullying and intimidation. This is workplace violence in action. Even sadder, this isn't likely an isolated case.

ACTION

Our **Action** phase becomes a little more challenging. What would you do in this situation?

Calley persevered until it got worse. She took action to resolve one aspect of her working conditions, which made it even worse. She eventually chose to leave the worksite. Economic necessity required her to return.

I will remind you that this is a practical guide to preventing and surviving violence in the workplace. Perhaps the most practical action that Calley could've taken was to quit this job shortly after she learned what the working conditions were like.

At the essence of this story is power and control. As the new hire, Calley had neither. Was Flo a bully? Most definitely! Were there other bullies at the worksite? The story doesn't specify so, however bully like behavior from her fellow staff seemed to be the norm rather than the exception.

When taking on a bully, your self-confidence can be a factor that determines the outcome. If you experience low self-esteem, low self-confidence, the bully will use it against you. However, as this manual is all about, knowledge is power, if you use it wisely. Many of the actions that could be used in this scenario can be drawn from the section on bullying outlined elsewhere in this manual.

Assuming that you have made the decision to stay and take on the bully and the dysfunctional worksite, here are some practical steps that you could take to do so. Feel free to add your own at any point.

1. Flo had an inordinate amount of power in the workplace, at least when she was on shift. Openly challenging her with other staff present would only fuel her attempts to maintain the upper hand. What about the other nurses and care-aides? Did they all back and support Flo or were there some that went along with her but didn't necessarily condone her behavior? When taking on a bully it is important to create alliances with your fellow workers. They may not have the courage to stand up on their own.
2. Documentation is the key to success when reporting an incident to your manager. It is nearly impossible for your manager to conduct an investigation when they are provided with anecdotal information. It is too easy for the bully to counter accuse or deny, saying that the events never happened or that your interpretation is biased. Collect objective facts. What did you see? Who was involved? Will any of those involved back up your story? When did the situation take place? Do not flavor your report with an opinion or add your interpretation of why the bully did what they did.
3. Familiarize yourself with the tactics that a bully will probably take when accused of wrong doing. There is great value in predicting a bully's actions.
4. If your worksite has a JOSH Committee (Joint Occupational Health & Safety), get the subject of working conditions placed on the agenda. It wouldn't necessarily be a good idea to address the bully by name, but there would be value in creating discussion on healthy and respectful workplaces.

CHAPTER 68
SECTION SEVEN SUMMARY:

This section has covered quite a bit of content and has likely stirred up some memories for you as you have read it, as it has for me to write it. I believe that it is important to keep in mind that many of the memories of traumatic incidents that we had in our childhood were retained or filed away in our vast computer of a brain with the state of development and/or the maturity, intelligence and the skills that we possessed at the time of the incident. We can't change the past, but we can learn from it.

The past has no power over us. A bully shouldn't wield that kind of control over our life either. Bullies, unfortunately, like the common cold, the flu and other common ailments, are out there. If you haven't encountered one yet, you are fortunate. You will in time.

In this section we identified what bullying is and why some people bully. We explored how to spot an employer that bullies. We learned how to regain control of our lives and the decisions that we make. We also learned practical steps that we can use to take the power away from a bully, and we looked at a couple of case scenarios that illustrated what we have learned.

In the next section we explore steps that we can take to prevent violence from a larger perspective, i.e. society in general. We will then apply it to our work settings and explore the value of working with others to prevent violence. Then we will learn methods to prevent disturbed behavior and identify influences for aggression in the clinical setting. We will also learn different actions that we can utilize to reduce or control aggression in our worksites. To end the chapter we will learn how to do a worksite assessment as a method of reducing aggression.

∽

SECTION EIGHT:
WHAT CAN I DO TO PREVENT AGGRESSION & VIOLENCE?

CHAPTER 69

PREVIEWING VIOLENCE -
INCREASE INDIVIDUAL
AWARENESS

ACTION

F ocusing on violence first... the bigger picture.

Preventing Violence - Increase Individual Awareness

Examine the root causes of violence and learn how the abuse of power and control leads to violence.

Learn how gender discrimination, racism, homophobia, and ageism are often present when violence takes place, and develop some strategies to challenge these dynamics.

Take A Stance Against Violence

Make a pledge never to commit, condone, or remain silent about violence.

Challenge beliefs that some people are better than others because of their age, race, cultural heritage, ancestry, income, size, gender, religion, sexual orientation, or physical and/or mental ability.

Challenge behaviors by speaking out against violence as a form of entertainment in movies, television shows, or advertisements.

Challenge attitudes that treat violence as a private matter between two people or family members.

Work With Others To Create Change

Develop policies that prevent violence from happening such as sexual harassment policies in the workplace and respecting differences' models in schools.

Change physical structures that allow violence to continue such as amending building codes, as well as increasing safety devices in parking garages, public buildings, and public transportation facilities.

Contribute to decision and policy-making processes so that prevention strategies are adopted by your local boards or municipality.

Change Social Structures

Focus your efforts on reducing power imbalances at your home, schools, workplace, and community.

Join a group working to reduce poverty, unemployment, or unequal opportunities.

Review your organization's policies, programs, or services to determine if they discriminate on the basis of gender, disability, sexual orientation, language, culture, or age.

Joint Occupational Health & Safety Committee (JOSH) Responsibilities

If you work in a unionized environment, you likely have a JOSH Committee at your worksite or perhaps at another if your organization has several sites. JOSH committees are composed of both managers and union members sitting at the table as equals to focus on OH&S

related issues. In nonunionized settings, an OH&S committee may also exist.

Overall, the OH&S committee's specific duties should include the following:

- Monitoring the violence in the workplace program by reviewing statistical information (risk assessment results, training records, incident reports, investigation reports etc.)
- Reviewing incidents of workplace violence and make recommendations for prevention strategies if necessary.
- Ensure that recommendations for prevention strategies are followed-up
- When appropriate and necessary, participate in investigations of incidents involving violence in the workplace
- Participate in program review

Adapted from Guidelines: Code White Response. A Component of Prevention and Management of Aggressive Behavior in Healthcare. In partnership with: OHSAH, WCB of British Columbia and the Health Association of B.C. 2002

Secondly, we focus on aggression in our worksites and how we can control and reduce it.

CHAPTER 70
EFFECTIVE PERSONAL ATTITUDES IN PREVENTING DISTURBED BEHAVIOR

These personal attitudes have been effective [by care-givers] when working with disturbed individuals:

- Genuineness
- Alertness
- Sensitiveness
- Self-awareness
- Confidence
- Respectfulness
- Belief in Equality

Preventing Disturbed Behaviour Quick List

ASK FOR HELP WHEN THE SITUATION MAY BE UNSAFE.

Make alert observations regarding unusual behavior and behavior patterns.

Report changes in behavior and refer problems to the correct person as necessary.

Talk to others using a calm approach and nonthreatening gestures.

Have good listening skills.

Be assertive.

Avoid power struggles.

Encourage win/win situations.

Understand the importance of face saving in conflict resolution.

Do not avoid the angry person.

Do not allow anger to direct your behavior.

Do not "take personally" someone's aggressive behavior.

Monitor prescribed medication.

When necessary, use a firm, consistent approach and set limits.

Interventions should be organized, well timed, and suitable for the situation.

A team approach is usually the most effective. Ask for help if in doubt.

As a group, try to evaluate the situation after an incident.

Interventions should be organized, well timed, and suitable for the situation.

CHAPTER 71
PREVENTING DISTURBED BEHAVIOR
ENVIRONMENTAL INFLUENCES

Quick List

Keep noise under control.

Try to remove the audience when someone is acting out.

Whenever possible increase: privacy, variety in activities, options in space, choices

Respect the need for personal space.

Avoid rigid, inflexible scheduling for bedtime, meal and bathing.

A predictable daily routine that is interesting and stimulating is a good combination.

Consider cleanliness, light, heat, ventilation, and decoration as factors that may contribute to disturbed behavior.

Decrease powerlessness and increase empowerment where possible.

Replace confusion with clarity.

Encourage coalition rather than isolation.

General prevention procedures, such as not giving out worker information over the phone and minimizing risks for violence in specific workplace locations such as the reception area.

Reinforce desired behaviors. Reinforcement techniques should concentrate on rewarding patients for the absence of physical confrontations rather than focusing on disruptive behaviors. For example, patients who have improved their behavior could earn community passes to leave the facility with family members.

A major intervention is to develop policies, procedures and skills that support empowerment, clarity, and coalition.

Complete a Workplace Assessment & Survey to determine the current safety level of the worksite. Visit https://BookHip.com/QJDCAH for a free downloadable workplace assessment form.

CHAPTER 72
PREVENTION AND MANAGEMENT OF AGGRESSION
QUICK LIST

Have you informed your coworkers that you will be dealing with a distraught client?

Have you provided a quiet, private environment, to reduce stimuli and interruptions? (Don't isolate yourself with a client who has a known history of violence. The room should be free of weapons or projectiles.)

Do you and your client have an exit from the room?

Are you maintaining a supportive position (at least 3 feet away), standing or sitting at an angle, palms open, arms uncrossed, casual eye contact, using a moderate tone of voice?)

Are you setting gentle, firm, enforceable limits to help the client to regain control?

Are you maintaining respect and empathy for the client and maintaining your objectivity? (Don't allow yourself to become angry, loud, or argumentative; also, don't promise more than you can deliver.)

CHAPTER 73
ACTIONS TO TAKE WITH SPECIFIC CLIENT GROUPS:

Action

Psychotic Client:

- Remove to a quiet, private area if not aggressive or hostile.
- Decrease stimulation.
- Listen carefully.
- Avoid premature interpretations.
- Orient to reality.
- Avoid reinforcing delusions or hallucinations but don't challenge them either.

- Interrupt hallucinations by having the client attend to what is happening.
- Assess content of hallucinations, are they command in nature?
- Make clear concise statements.
- Limit choices as client has difficulty making decisions.
- Share your information about client's increased agitation with other staff members.
- Use PRN medication if permitted.

Depressed Client:

- Use a warm, accepting, empathetic approach.
- Remove to quiet area to give the client full attention and help to retain self-respect.
- Ask how you can help.
- Allow the client time to respond.
- Evaluate the client's potential for suicide.
- Use open-ended questions.
- Label the affect (sad, angry, frustrated) and encourage verbalization of same.
- Reassure the client that he/she is safe and that he/she will be helped to maintain control.
- Encourage relaxation techniques or participation in activities.

Hypo-manic Client:

- Give simple, truthful responses.
- Set constructive limits on negative behavior— avoid confrontation.
- Use a consistent approach by all staff members.
- Reinforce the client's self-control and positive aspects of behavior.

- Remove to a quiet environment to reduce stimuli.
- Focus on the present situation-- not past or future.
- Speak clearly and concisely.
- Share your knowledge with other staff that client is escalating and administer PRN medication.
- Don't isolate yourself with a client who has a known history of violence.
- Allow choices but be specific.
- Encourage constructive expression of feelings.
- Don't allow yourself to become angry, loud or argue.
- Don't promise more that you can deliver.
- Don't imply punishment for anger.

Intervention Techniques to Interrupt Hallucinations

- Establish a trusting, interpersonal relationship.
- Look and listen for cues (symptoms) and evidence of the hallucination.
- Focus on the cue and elicit the individual's observation and description.
- Identify if the hallucination is emotional or chemical-based.
- If asked, point out simply that you are not experiencing the same stimuli. Follow the direction of the individual and help him or her observe and describe the present and recently past hallucination. Elicit the individual's observation of past hallucinations.
- Encourage the individual to observe and describe thoughts, feelings, and actions, both present and past, as they relate to the hallucination.
- Help the person see if a correlation between the hallucination and the need it is serving exists.
- Suggest and reinforce the individual's use of increased interpersonal relationships in meeting the need.
- Focus on other and related aspects of the individual's psychopathological behavior.

ALZHEIMER PATIENTS

Communicating with the person with Alzheimer's disease is a challenge. In order to keep them in touch with the people around them, you will have to try to make up for their failing abilities.

Knowing how to communicate is important. You need to use different ways of getting your message across, because the person gradually becomes less able to express their ideas in words and less able to understand what is said to them.

Gentle touch, body movements, expressions on your face, and tone of your voice can all convey messages to which a person with Alzheimer's Disease may respond. At the same time, the person can "speak" to you by actions and expressions when they are no longer able to use words well.

Communication requires patience and imagination. The following guide-lines may help you:

1) **Set the Stage:** Communication is always easier if other things are not happening at the same time. Keep your environment quiet and calm. For example, a TV or radio is distracting to the person with Alzheimer's --- turn it off.

2) **Get Their Attention:** Approach the person slowly and from the front. Gently touch the person's hand or arm to help get their attention. Don't start talking until you know they are ready to listen.

3) **Make Eye Contact:** If possible, sit facing them or stand in front of them and keep eye contact. This makes it easier for them to understand what you are saying.

4) **SPEAK SLOWLY AND CLEARLY:** USE SIMPLE WORDS AND SHORT sentences. Speak clearly and slowly. If the person has hearing problems, face them and lower the pitch of your voice.

. . .

5) Give One Message at a Time: Keep conversations simple. Do not include too many thoughts or ideas at one time. Do not give many choices. Questions which can be answered with "yes" or "no" are easier than open-ended questions. "Would you like soup for lunch?" is easier to answer than "What would you like for lunch?"

6) Pay Attention: Their reactions to what you say can give you some idea of how much they are understanding. Pay attention to the expressions on their face. Respond to their moods and feelings when the words they use are wrong or inappropriate.

7) Repeat Important Information: If the person has not understood the message the first time, repeat it, using the same words.

8) Show and Talk: Show them what you mean as well as telling them. For example, if it is time to wash their hair, have the shampoo and towel at hand to help you explain.

CHAPTER 74
RISK ASSESSMENT

What is a risk assessment?

Risk assessment is a step-by-step look at the workplace and work process to:

- Determine what violence prevention measures are already in place
- Identify potentially hazardous conditions, operations, activities, and situations that could contribute to workplace violence
- Determine the risk of future violent incidents, using the above information

WHAT ACTIVITIES SHOULD BE INCLUDED IN THE RISK ASSESSMENT?

CONDUCTING A THOROUGH RISK ASSESSMENT INCLUDES THE following activities:

- **Gathering background information:** An information review is a systematic look at information about violent incidents and their prevention in the workplace. Questions to ask include: how often have violent incidents occurred, how severe were they, does any pattern(s) emerge, can any triggers to the events be identified, are there any policies & procedures in place to address violent behavior, are there any arrangements in place already to prevent violent incidents and what follow-up actions need to be taken as a result of the answers to these questions.
- Obtaining staff input
- Inspecting the workplace
- Analyzing the information
- Recording and communicating results

THE FINAL STEP IS TO DESIGNATE A LEVEL OF RISK. BECAUSE NOT ALL workers are equally at risk for violence and not all factors create the same degree of risk, it is important to have a process of identifying individuals and areas of greatest risk. A common scale used is, high risk, moderate risk or low risk. The explanation of the categories would seem to be self-explanatory.

Adapted from Preventing Violence in Health Care: Five Steps to an Effective Program. Worksafe B.C., 2000

CHAPTER 75
SECTION EIGHT SUMMARY:

In this section we explored steps we can take to prevent violence from a larger perspective i.e. society in general. Then we applied it to our work settings. We explored the value of working with others to prevent violence. We then learned methods to prevent disturbed behavior and identify influences for aggression in the clinical setting. We also learned different actions that we can utilize to reduce or control aggression in our worksites. In conclusion we learned how to do a worksite assessment as a method of reducing aggression.

IN SECTION NINE WE EXPLORE COMMUNICATION SKILLS AS UTILIZED by the FBI. We will be offered some practical exercises to develop our communication skills and explore the rationale behind why and how a particular technique works. We will also explore pitfalls in communication i.e. those that take away from effective communication. We will conclude with an exploration of personal qualities, attributes that relate to violence in the workplace.

SECTION NINE:
COMMUNICATION SKILLS

CHAPTER 76
COMMUNICATION SKILLS

Action

A thorough exploration of communication skills one would use in maintaining a therapeutic relationship is beyond the scope of this publication. The reader is advised to research authors with more experience than myself. However, having said that, it is important at this juncture to explore some specific communication techniques that have been identified as being beneficial in preventing and diffusing crises.

. . .

I WOULD SUGGEST THAT YOU ACCESS A HELPFUL ARTICLE THAT IS currently on the internet that addresses effective communication techniques to utilize in a volatile situation.

Law Enforcement Bulletin - August 1997
Crisis Intervention: Using Active Listening Skills in Negotiations
By Gary W. Noesner, M. Ed. and Mike Webster, Ed. D.

THE COMPLETE ARTICLE IS AVAILABLE AT HTTP://WWW.WSHNA.COM/ yahoo_site_admin/assets/docs/ Active_Listening_Skills__Webster__Noesner_.307125550.pdf

ACCORDING TO GARY W. NOESNER, M. ED. AND MIKE WEBSTER, Ed. D., the FBI and a growing number of law enforcement agencies in recent years have used active listening to resolve volatile confrontations successfully. These positive results have led the FBI to incorporate and emphasize active listening skills in its crisis negotiation training. The following seven techniques constitute the core elements of the active listening approach the FBI teaches. Together, these techniques provide a framework for negotiators to respond to the immediate emotional needs of expressive subjects, clearing the way for behavioral changes that must occur before negotiators can resolve critical incidents.

ASSUMING YOU HAVE REFERENCED AND READ THE ABOVE ARTICLE, WE have learned about the benefits of utilizing effective communication skills from a law enforcement perspective. Now we will peel back another layer from our metaphorical onion and look at it from another

perspective, a clinical one. Practical exercises have been added should you wish to actively improve your skills.

Paraphrasing: As we have discovered, an important skill in interviewing is the ability to paraphrase. Paraphrasing is giving back the client's meaning of a phrase or sentence in your own words. Paraphrasing is similar to *reflection* in that it is focused on the client's inner process. The major difference is that while reflection attends to feelings, paraphrasing attempts to capture the *meaning* of what was communicated, be it cognitive or affective.

By using your own words, you are accomplishing two important tasks. First, you are translating the client's words into your own thoughts. Second, you are checking out the translation with the client. This gives the client the opportunity to verify your "translation" and to think further about the matter at hand.

One question that continually arises about paraphrasing is "How much do I change the words around?" Unfortunately, there is no hard and fast answer. A partial guideline lies in the answer to the following question: "How can I rephrase this, so it is in my own words?" The answer to this question will vary depending on the nurse, the client, and the context, which are, after all, the three parts of any communication.

An example of paraphrasing occurs in the following interaction:

Client: "I've had the arthritis for a long time but it doesn't seem to get any worse."

. . .

NURSE: "SO, ALTHOUGH YOU'VE HAD IT QUITE A WHILE, IT'S ABOUT the same?"

NOTICE THE NURSE REPHRASES "DOESN'T SEEM TO GET ANY WORSE" to "it's about the same," which is a reasonable choice. If the rephrasing had been "it's probably better" or "it's hard to tell if it changes," it would not have been a good paraphrase, even if the client agreed, because the nurse expanded the client's meaning. Paraphrasing thus becomes a tool to be used carefully because it can be used to enhance or distort the client's meaning.

QUESTIONS ARE USED TO ELICIT RESPONSES WITH RESPECT TO THE following points:

1. TO DESCRIBE AND ELABORATE PERCEPTIONS, IDEAS, AND FEELINGS
2. To clarify perceptions, ideas, and feelings
3. To validate observations
4. To substantiate facts
5. To assess the reliability of the information received
6. To interpret the meaning of a group of facts
7. To compare information with some predetermined criteria
8. To formulate solutions based on previous assessments and comparisons
9. To evaluate the outcome of a plan or action

OPEN-ENDED QUESTIONS

. . .

We all use a variety of ways to set the tone and control the direction of our interviews with patients. Some of us arrange the chairs, adjust the lighting, and see that privacy is ensured. These are important steps, which are an initial part of the interview. The questions we employ also set the tone and control the direction of our interviews with patients. Open-ended questions are well-suited for initiating interviews because they do not restrict a patient's responses or confine him to a specific topic. He can respond in his own way to such questions, and it is from his individualistic response that we can begin to determine his attitudes and feelings, as well as to plan other questions that begin to touch upon his concerns.

The preliminary open-ended question provides us with the opportunity to observe how the other person responds verbally and nonverbally to the information disclosed. These opportunities assist us in assessing the type and level of vocabulary used by the patient as he discusses a situation, event, or idea. Because open-ended questions elicit responses that are more than one or two words in length, they are well-suited to situations in which descriptive, elaborative, or comparative responses are needed. During these expanded responses the nurse can often determine the importance of the event to the patient, the chronological order of events, and the patient's frame of reference for his observation of or participation in the event.

There are other advantages to using open-ended questions with patients in the interview. Through them, we convey more than just the question. We convey the feeling that we care about him, care about his thoughts and feelings, and care about the things he has to say, because his well-being is important to us.

The question and the interest and sincerity conveyed in it increase the patient's willingness to respond in a helpful, contributing manner but do not force him to divulge information or recall an event before he is ready to do so. The feeling of having to supply an answer can be threatening to a patient and therefore inhibit his responses or force him to make up answers that will please us. The open-ended question allows him to verbalize in his own way. Given the opportunity, patients often voice their doubts and fears, as well as assist themselves in answering their own questions and in making their own decisions.

THE PATIENT'S RESPONSE TO OPEN-ENDED QUESTIONS PERMITS US TO detect discrepancies or gaps in information. The knowledge supplied can be assessed and used to plan further questions that will give a more complete picture of his thoughts and feelings relative to his concerns and his nursing care.

THOUGH OPEN-ENDED QUESTIONS ALLOW PATIENTS FREEDOM OF response, they should be posed thoughtfully. Too many such questions or their exclusive use may cause the interview to be side-tracked by irrelevant topics. Overuse may also create confusion in both participants by clouding the original topic or point under discussion. With the abundance of information we can receive, we may have difficulty reflecting on the original topic or goals set for the interview. In addition, the information given in response to an open-ended question may , in some instances be difficult to sort out.

FROM THE PRACTICE AND REFINEMENT OF COMMUNICATION SKILLS by health professionals in interview situations, have come some common words that have proved useful not only in constructing open-ended questions but also in facilitating the communication of our clients. The words who, what, where, when and how, if used to introduce thoughtfully planned questions, guide communication. These words are used only when a situation necessitates their use. They can also serve as a guide by which we can evaluate the effectiveness or our efforts to facilitate a partner's communication. They are valid when uses thoughtfully and with due consideration for their purpose. Some examples of open-ended questions that illustrate this point are:

TO DESCRIBE AND ELABORATE PERCEPTIONS, IDEAS, AND FEELINGS.

"What happened at your daughter's last night?"

"What did she say that caused you to be upset?"

2) TO COMPARE THE INFORMATION WITH SOME PREDETERMINED criteria, such as nursing goals.

"How does your former neighborhood in Vancouver compare to your one here in Kelowna?" "In which way did your father's behavior differ from your last visit?"

3) TO FORMULATE SOLUTIONS BASED ON PREVIOUS ASSESSMENTS AND comparisons.

"What plans have you made for your care when you leave the hospital?"

"How might you deal with the situation if it should occur again?"

4) TO ASSESS THE RELIABILITY OF THE INFORMATION RECEIVED.

"What happened just before you got the headache?"

"How many minutes went by between the time you asked for pain medication and when you received it?"

5) TO EVALUATE THE OUTCOME OF A PLAN OR ACTION.

"What made your last visit to the senior center so enjoyable?"

"What do you feel helped you do better on your last test?"

EXERCISE FOR OPEN-ENDED AND FOCUSED QUESTIONS

FORM INTO GROUPS OF THREE - ONE WILL BE A, B, C

A will be a client

B will be a staff

C will be an observer

* Make up a scenario.

B WILL BEGIN THE DIALOGUE WITH OPEN-ENDED QUESTIONS, followed by a few focused questions.

AT THE END OF TWO MINUTES, **C** WILL TELL **B** HOW **B** DID.

SWITCH ROLES UNTIL ALL HAVE HAD A CHANCE.

DISCUSS HOW FOCUSED QUESTIONS HELPED TO ADDRESS THE ISSUES AT hand.

PROBING

A PROBE IS ANY QUESTION OR STATEMENT USED TO PURSUE FURTHER detail about an area. Thus, focused questions also constitute a beginning probe. Any other phrase, question, or remark the nurse makes to gain further information on the same topic is a probe. Probes can be open-ended, focused or closed-ended.

Some standard probes include:

"Tell me more."

"Can you tell me more?"

"Is there anything you left out?"

"How do you feel about that?"

"... and"

"Um-humm" (followed by silence)

Probes have to be handled very carefully, so they do not seem to be an invasion of the client's sense of privacy. It takes a great deal of practice and sensitivity to be able to determine how far and how much to probe. If you see the client tensing up or hear defensiveness in the client's voice, it may be time to reflect or to leave the probe until the client is more relaxed.

Probing Exercise

Pair up. One will be **A**, the other **B**.

A will give **B** a few sentences about an imaginary health or psychosocial problem.

B then responds with a probe.

A then answers the probe. After the answer, **A** will tell **B** how the probe felt, how it could have been improved, etc.

Switch roles--do several times.

DISCUSS THE REASONS FOR AND AGAINST PURSUING (PROBING) ISSUES that are discomforting for the client.

Reflection

RELATED TO PARAPHRASING IS THE USE OF REFLECTION. INSTEAD OF focusing on the content, however, reflection acknowledges the affective aspects of the message. Reflection underscores the emotional component of the client's message by calling the client's attention to the underlying feelings associated with the content. In using this strategy, the purpose is to help the client clarify important feelings and to experience them with their appropriate intensity in relation to a particular situation or event.

Factors to Consider in Using Reflection

- Timing
- Hackneyed overuse
- Distorting the client's communication by adding or subtracting from the client's feelings

TIMING IS CRITICAL IN THE USE OF REFLECTION. ENOUGH OF THE client's message should be available for processing the attitudes and feelings the client may be experiencing. Reflection will have more impact if it is used to accentuate only the more important themes. Using the statement "You feel" after each client statement suggests a shallow approach rather than genuine listening. The interviewer should be sensitive to the client's readiness to discuss feelings and attitudes. Otherwise, the listening response will appear lacking in feeling or purpose, despite the "feeling" words that are used.

. . .

Connecting feeling with content is valuable in the expansion of the client's full understanding of therapeutic self-care demands. Emotional responses, however, generally are more difficult for clients to assimilate. For this reason, reflection generally is used after initial rapport is developed with the client.

The goals of this technique are threefold:

1) To encourage the client to become aware of the feelings while at the same time implicitly giving the client permission to have them.

2) To encourage the client to express more of his or her feelings.

3) To increase the client's understanding of the connection between situational experiences and their affective components.

Examples of reflection include the following:

- "You sound really frustrated."
- "It sounds as if you are pretty angry your mother didn't visit."
- "What I think I hear you saying is that you feel guilty because you weren't home at the time of the accident?"

Silence

. . .

SILENCE, USED DELIBERATELY AND JUDICIOUSLY, IS A POWERFUL communication technique. When a client communicates a message, it sometimes is beneficial to step back momentarily and mentally process what you think you heard before responding. The chances of responding appropriately are enhanced by giving careful attention to the essence of the communicated message. Too often a quick response addresses only a small part of the message or gives the client an insufficient opportunity to fully formulate a complete idea. On the other hand, a silence that lingers too long becomes uncomfortable.

THE SILENT PAUSE SHOULD BE JUST THAT, A BRIEF DISCONNECTION followed by a verbal comment. Being silent does not mean that the interviewer tunes the client out or has nothing to say. Silence should be purposeful. It can be used therapeutically to:

1) ALLOW THE CLIENT TO PROCESS INFORMATION AND TO CARRY ON an internal dialogue. (This technique is particularly useful in elderly clients and those from foreign cultures.)

2) GIVES THE INTERVIEWER AND CLIENT TIME TO SEARCH FOR WORDS to describe feelings or situations.

3) CONVEY THE SHARED MEANINGFULNESS OF A DIFFICULT emotional situation.

4) ENCOURAGE THE CLIENT TO RESPOND VERBALLY.

5) ASSESS NONVERBAL CUES, INCLUDING THE CLIENT'S LEVEL OF anxiety.

. . .

Silence also may be used to accent an important point in a verbal communication. By pausing briefly after presenting a key idea, before proceeding to the next one, the interviewer encourages the client's use of the most important elements of the communication. Used prudently, a brief silence following an important verbal message dramatizes the significance of the interviewer's statement.

Clarifying

Often, a client will say or do something in the course of an interview the nurse does not understand. When this occurs, there is an immediate question of judgment that has to be answered: "Do I need to understand this now?" If the answer is you do, then a request for clarification is appropriate. Other choices can include requesting clarification later on (especially if the client is quite upset and not listening too well) or in a subsequent interview.

If the request for clarification is presented with warmth and empathy, it is likely to be perceived by the client as a sign of interest and an honest attempt to create understanding. The tone of voice used with a clarification response should be neutral, not accusatory or demanding. It also "models" asking for clarification, and hopefully the client can use the same skill with the interviewer.

Failure to ask for clarification when part of the communication is poorly understood means that the nurse will act on incomplete or inaccurate information.

There are many ways to request clarification. Some examples are as follows:

. . .

"I'm not sure I understand that completely. Could you repeat it?"

"I missed the last few words you said."

"I don't follow you. Can you say it another way?"

"Do you mean that... [repeat client's message]?"

Clarification Exercise

Pair up. One will be **A** the other **B**.

A will be the helper.

B will be the client.

B will say a couple of statements to confuse **A**.

A will attempt to clarify.

Repeat a few times, then switch.

Share experience from the pairs, including the most confusing statements and listing all ways members of the group seek clarification.

CHAPTER 77
PITFALLS IN COMMUNICATION:

I said we weren't going to explore communication skills in depth but indulge me a little further. Just as important as using effective, therapeutic communication skills is that of not using counterproductive communication techniques. The following is a compendium of techniques that you should *avoid*.

1) ADVICE GIVING

2) Blaming the client

3) Changing the topic inappropriately

4) Defensiveness

5) False reassurance

6) Judging the client

7) Leading statements

8) Moralizing

9) Multiple questions

10) Overuse of closed-ended questions

11) Parroting (instead of reflection)

12) Patronizing the client

13) Placating the client

14) Rationalizing feelings

15) Stumped silence

16) "Why" questions

Pitfall 1: Advice Giving

GIVING ADVICE ON ADVICE GIVING IS RELATIVELY SIMPLE: DON'T! There are several reasons for limiting advice giving in a clinical setting. The first is the advice generally will not be taken. The second is that if the client "takes it to heart," the helper who gave the advice may be blamed if anything goes wrong. And the third reason is clients are likely to misinterpret the advice and not follow it carefully.

WHAT EXACTLY IS ADVICE? THE DICTIONARY DEFINES IT AS AN opinion. When clients ask helpers for an opinion or advice about what to do, the helper may well (inadvertently) set him-or herself up to take inappropriate responsibility for clients' decisions. If it is a question of an "informal helper opinion," helpers can use the tactic of giving clients information and exploring options as opposed to giving advice. The client is viewed as an active participant in the health process; for this reason the giving of advice is not advocated.

Pitfall 2: Blaming the Client

. . .

BLAME CARRIES WITH IT DECREASED SELF-REGARD FOR THE CLIENT who is directly or indirectly being told "It's your fault". However, there is a subtle but important distinction between blame and responsibility.

CLIENTS CAN BE RESPONSIBLE FOR MANY ASPECTS OF THEIR OWN health and well-being. They can be educated as to how certain aspects of their lives led up to their current state of health (eating, exercise, job pressure, drinking, etc.). When the educational aspect turns into a put-down and an implied message of accusation, then the client will feel blamed and guilty and experience lowered self-worth. Along with these nontherapeutic aspects of blaming, most psychological research has demonstrated that simple punishment — for example, blaming—is not an effective way to change behavior. What happens is that only certain patterns of behavior change, the client will stop making appointments for example. In this way, the client avoids blame or punishment.

BLAME CAN ALSO COME UNDER THE GUISE OF ADVICE. THERE ARE AN infinite number of ways to blame the client. Some are obvious, some are not. Many are unintended. Some examples of blame are:

"WELL, YOU SHOULD HAVE CALLED EARLIER TO MAKE AN appointment."

"Don't you know that smoking is bad?"

"You're supposed to eat everything on your plate."

"Look, we told you to take your medication three times a day. What's the matter with you?"

ONE WAY TO WORK ON BLAMING BEHAVIOR IS FIRST IDENTIFYING IT in ourselves and then transforming it into a message that indicates respect for ourselves as well as clients.

Pitfall 3: Changing Topic Inappropriately

A third common pitfall in helper communication is the inappropriate change of topic by the helper. Generally, helpers change topics inappropriately more as a result of their own rising anxiety than for reasons specifically related to clients. Thus the change of topic is inappropriate in that it is not a strategy that helps clients.

If helpers find themselves inappropriately changing topics while interviewing clients, an investigation of the following areas might help to suggest the source of their anxiety.

- The client is touching on a topic area which the helper feels uncomfortable (sex, emotional problems).
- The helper is unsure of what to do and is uncomfortable just listening.
- The client is describing a problem that exists for the helper.
- The helper is embarrassed by what the client says.

Pitfall 4: Defensiveness

Defensiveness is a more general category than many of the other pitfalls reviewed in this section. Defensiveness is defined as "being hostile, aggressive, not listening, or responding as if one had been attacked." Helpers who have a defensive approach to clients usually indicate it in their words and nonverbal behavior. It is difficult, if not impossible, to be empathetic, listen well, and give messages of reassurance when one is feeling defensive.

. . .

However, there are times when any helper will feel defensive, be it triggered by something that happened at home, on the job, or during the interview. There are two schools of thought on what to do at these times. One is to finish the interview as if "nothing is the matter" and then work things through with a peer or your supervisor.

The second school of thought is to comment on one's emotional state briefly to the client. This choice gives the client some understanding about how you, the helper, are acting, and it can model comments about feelings from the client, which can be therapeutic. Examples of how to acknowledge your own defensiveness briefly include:

"I feel somewhat uncomfortable about this topic but I am listening to you carefully."

"I want to let you know I'm upset by other things today. Please do not take my reactions as a statement about you."

There are reasons to share and not share one's own defensiveness with clients. The reasons for sharing include the following:

- Models self-disclosure
- Explains own behavior
- Can build trust
- Helps helper to get over defensiveness

THE REASONS FOR **NOT** SHARING ONE'S DEFENSIVENESS INCLUDE THE following:

- Client could be overwhelmed
- It could be taken as a sign of weakness or incompetence
- The helper could end up "being the client"
- Clients can feel pressured into disclosing things they are not ready to disclose

PITFALL 5: FALSE REASSURANCE

ONE OF THE GREAT TEMPTATIONS TO ANY HELPER IS TO "LIGHTEN the emotional load" of a distressed client. Ways in which an effective helper communicator can give appropriate verbal and nonverbal reassurance have already been discussed. However, there are times when, with good intentions, the helper gives false reassurance. That is, in trying to reassure the client, the helper promises something that may not happen, says something that is untrue, or provides comfort in an incongruent manner. Examples of the three forms of false reassurance are:

1) PROMISING SOMETHING THAT MAY NOT HAPPEN: "DON'T WORRY. Everything will be all right."

2) SAYING SOMETHING NOT TRUE: "YOU HAVE NOTHING TO WORRY about."

3) GIVING INCONGRUENT COMFORT: "I FEEL FOR YOU" (WHEN IN actuality, the helper is trying to figure out what to do next).

False reassurance may raise client's anxiety. Rather than being reassured, the client will become suspicious and more concerned as the inconsistency in the message from the helper is noted. By consistency, we mean that either the helper's message is incongruent, or it is inconsistent with the client's perception of the problem.

Pitfall 6: Judging the Client

Judging the client incorporates any tendencies the helper has to evaluate the client as being "good" or "bad." In general practice, more emphasis is put on negative evaluation of the client than positive evaluation. However, even positive evaluation (as opposed to unconditional positive regard) can have problems. For example, if helpers are in the habit of nodding their heads and saying "that's good" during an interview when they hear things they like, clients will quickly learn to tell only those things that get rewarded and they may leave out pertinent information concerning their health.

There is an important distinction that needs to be made between evaluating behavior and evaluating the client. For example, it is quite appropriate to tell a client that a self-administered procedure was done incorrectly. That is your job. However, there can be negative consequences if the message carries with it a negative judgment of the client as well. Most clients respond to "being judged" by becoming uncooperative.

A client can feel judged by seeing a raised eyebrow, a "stern" look, hearing a raised voice, or by being blamed. In all fairness, clients may feel judged even when no judgment is intended or made. However, because the client is likely to be extremely sensitive to judgment, it is important to take note of all the ways helpers can judge the client and work on developing nonjudgmental communication.

Pitfall 7: Leading Statements

A COMMON MISTAKE OF BEGINNING INTERVIEWERS IS TO "PUT WORDS in the client's mouth" or make a leading statement. A leading statement is anyone that indirectly makes the interviewer's interpretation or observation appear to be the client's. Several examples include:

"YOU'RE TIRED BECAUSE YOU'RE DEPRESSED, RIGHT?"

"You probably forgot the appointment because you were worried about the holidays."

"It doesn't hurt too much, does it?"

THE PROBLEM WITH A LEADING STATEMENT IS THAT IT DOES NOT give the client a full opportunity to decide if it is true or not, especially if the client is under stress.

Pitfall 8: Moralizing

MORALIZING IS A SPECIFIC FORM OF JUDGING THE CLIENT. Moralizing refers to any instance in which helpers judge clients based on their own personal values. Examples of moralizing statements include:

"HOW CAN YOU SMOKE AT YOUR AGE?"

"Why do you eat sugar when you are overweight?"

"Abortion is sinful!"

"Abortion is OK for everyone"

A good question for consideration is: "How can I be an effective helper with someone whose values differ significantly from mine on the issue at hand?"

Pitfall 9: Multiple Questions

A less emotionally charged pitfall is use of multiple questions. Multiple questions are really a series of questions that are asked as if they are one question.

For example:

"Did you forget the appointment or did you have something else or did you call me and the line was busy?"

"Where do you live-- is it an apartment and what is your neighborhood like?"

Multiple questions are difficult to answer. Clients, especially when distressed, can get confused as to which question should be answered first. Many multiple questions get asked because the helper is somewhat anxious and does not give the client adequate time to think of a response. The helper assumes that the client is having a problem figuring out the question, and without checking it out, asks another question (or two). The result can be confusing.

. . .

Any multiple question can be broken down into separate single questions that can then be posed to the client. In other words, helpers can ask one question at a time and wait for the client to respond before rephrasing or asking another question.

Pitfall 10: Overuse of Closed-Ended Questions

As mentioned earlier, closed-ended questions elicit one or two word responses. Obviously, there are certain closed-ended questions that are appropriate, such as requests for specific information (name, address, names of medications.). However, these direct questions can be overused when the purpose of the communication is to open up a new area or probe further into a relatively unexplored one.

By overusing closed-ended questions, the helper becomes an interrogator, puts the client on the defensive, and has to do most of the talking. Except in the case where there is a check-list of items to be asked, open-ended questions, such as "Tell me about your medication," followed by appropriate focused and occasionally closed-ended probes can be a more effective approach.

Pitfall 11: Parroting

"Parroting" refers to the continual repetition of parts of the client's phrases as an attempt to reflect or paraphrase. While occasional repetition of portions of the phrases is effective in highlighting aspects, the helper would like the client to pursue, the overuse of this technique makes the helper seem like a parrot, mechanically repeating whatever is said.

Pitfall 12: Patronizing the Client

Often, nurses and other health professional talk to elderly clients as children in an overly kind manner, as if the client needed to be "talked down to" or put on a lower level than the helper or nurse. It is not so much a matter of words but how the words are said that gives the impression that clients are being treated as if they were less than human. The words and voice tones are not hostile; but they are, if anything, too sweet.

Patronizing the client refers to any and all ways the client is talked down to while being comforted. Several communication patterns that go along with patronizing the client include the helper keeping his or her eye level higher than that of the client (for example, standing while the client is sitting), talking in a sing-song voice, using "we" when either "you" or "I" is meant. And using (for lack of a better term) "baby talk" words, phrases, or voice tone.

The results of patronization are lowered self-worth and increased dependence (or anger) by the client. There is no valid reason to patronize a client. Even though the helper may be patronizing unintentionally, all clients deserve to be treated as equals in the interaction.

Pitfall 13: Placating the Client

A pitfall that is related to patronizing is placating. Placating the client means that the helper agrees with everything, takes the blame for everything, and cannot say no. Placation does not mean unconditional positive regard for the client.

The results of placating the client include decreased self-worth for the helper, as well as either dependence or anger on the part of the client. However, the temptation to placate can exist when it is easier to say yes to a demanding client than to say no and having to defend oneself.

Pitfall 14: Rationalizing Feelings

Rationalizing feelings means finding an apparently reasonable excuse for having the feelings. In fact, the excuse is not reasonable; it is an attempt to explain away whatever is being felt. This form of pitfall is a result of being "superreasonable" at a moment in time.

[Superreasonableness is a defensive communication style that serves to protect the self from uncomfortable feelings.]

The problem with rationalization is that feelings and behavior are subtly dismissed (e.g. "I only did that because..."). Rationalization also eliminates some unpleasant truths about the motivation for behavior in an interview. However, to rationalize the avoidance of a sensitive topic clouds the reason for discontinuing, since it may be the helper's problem, not the client's.

Pitfall 15: Stumped Silence

A stumped silence occurs when the client and the helper are both stuck. There is an uncomfortable feeling that nothing is going on, that the helper is confused.

A general guide in the instance of stumped silence is to metacomment about the confusion. That is, the helper can comment about being confused, which can then lead to the client's focusing on his or her own confusion.

Examples of appropriate comments to break a stumped silence are:

"I'm having trouble figuring out what to do next. How are you feeling?"

"At times it's hard to know what exactly to say. Let's see if we can continue in a few seconds."

Pitfall 16: "Why" Questions

One of the greatest temptations when a client says virtually anything is to respond, "Why did you say that?" The problem with "why" questions is that they imply that clients should come up with the underlying motivation of actions or feelings, which is what the helper usually wants. In addition, many clients will feel that the helper knows and is testing them. They then get into the guessing what the helper thinks rather than examining their own motivation. "Why" questions can also easily be asked or perceived as accusatory. For example:

"Why do you feel that way?"

"Why is the bandage off?"

"Why were you late?"

Almost any question can be rephrased as a less accusatory and more accurate statement. In the first of the examples given above, the helper may really be asking for more information about the client's thoughts. A more accurate question would be, "what are some thoughts behind that feeling?" or more simply, "Tell me more about it." The second example could have been rephrased: "What happened to the bandage?" and the third could have been stated as, "You were late. What happened?" As a general rule, try to avoid "Why" questions when interviewing clients.

~

CHAPTER 78
PERSONAL QUALITIES/ATTITUDES/APPROACHES

AWARENESS

We cannot accept responsibility for the disturbed or aggressive behavior of others.

"Violence can happen anywhere, at any time, to anyone, and under any circumstances... Even with the most appropriate intervention by staff members, violent behavior may still occur."

It is very important that staff not blame themselves or each other for the undesirable or disturbed behavior. E.g. "I wouldn't put up with that nonsense on my shift."

If blame is attached, or assumed, people become defensive, less objective, and less effective.

Remember, the goal is to "intervene effectively in order to provide for the best care and safety of the clients and staff."

Crisis Prevention Institute — National Report, Vol. 6, No. 1, 1986

CHAPTER 79
SECTION NINE SUMMARY:

In this section we explored communication skills utilized by the FBI. We were offered some practical exercises to develop our communication skills and the rationale behind why and how a particular technique works. We also explored pitfalls in communication, i.e. those that take away from effective communication. We concluded with an exploration of personal qualities, attributes that relate to violence in the workplace.

Our next section will be the conclusion.

SECTION TEN:
CONCLUSION

CHAPTER 80
CONCLUSION

Some authors will tell you that the best time to write your conclusion is at the beginning, when you first start and then write your story up to that point. The problem for me is that there really isn't an ending. The ending to this manual needs to be written by you.

For many of you I would suspect this book has been very much like one from the popular Dummies series of books i.e. telling you what you already know but repackaging it in a form that makes sense.

If this has been merely a good review for you, then I haven't met my objectives. On the other hand, if I have introduced you to a new concept or strengthened your resolve to rid our workplaces of violence, then I have met my objectives.

For those of you who are new to the healthcare field and/or have been fortunate not to have experienced workplace violence firsthand, this book may have been an eye-opener for you.

I have tried not to inundate you with "war" stories. Every nurse has their own litany of stories that have caused them severe distress.

My credo early in my career was that of Conan the Barbarian "What doesn't kill you... makes you stronger!" As I grew older and more self-confident, I decided that was somewhat of a negative attitude. While not being killed is certainly desirable, the goal isn't necessarily to be stronger. The goal is to be smarter for the next time. To learn what went right and what went wrong in every situation.

I quoted William Feathers earlier as saying "Knowledge is power". Together, we have explored the subject of workplace violence in our healthcare field. We need to take the next step and make it a higher profile in our worksites. If we don't, who will? Knowledge is only power if we share it with others and bring them along with us on the journey.

It would be an unfair generalization for me to say that employers are shirking their responsibilities in providing their employees with adequate training in workplace violence prevention. Many are. Note the word "adequate" though.

While many geographical regions have workers compensation legislation in place that has language addressing workplace violence prevention, "adequate" can often be interpreted as "minimal."

Watching a video or taking a two-hour workshop doesn't develop the skills you need to be proficient in violence awareness and prevention. Responding to a violent situation or defusing a potentially violent one shouldn't be any different from responding to a fire drill. We practice fire drills regularly. We know what to do in an emergency automatically because we have practiced it over and over. Why should responding to a crisis in our worksite be any different? We need to practice those skills often so that they are there when we need them.

It is very easy to get complacent. "It won't happen to me." "We haven't had an incident in years." Just because your worksite hasn't experienced an incident, it doesn't mean it won't. As workload pressures and working short-handed increase, we can expect to see an increase in worker to worker conflict. Like a pressure cooker heating up, the pressure has to release itself somehow.

Here is something to think about... the workplace violent episode or injury that you prevent may very well be your own! Will you be prepared when it happens to you?

ABOUT THE AUTHOR

Rae A. Stonehouse is a Canadian born author & speaker.

His professional career as a Registered Nurse working predominantly in psychiatry/mental health, has spanned four decades.

Rae has embraced the principal of CANI (Constant and Never-ending Improvement) as promoted by thought leaders such as Tony Robbins and brings that philosophy to each of his publications and presentations.

Rae has dedicated the latter segment of his journey through life to overcoming his personal inhibitions. As a 25+ year member of Toastmasters International he has systematically built his self-confidence and communicating ability.

He is passionate about sharing his lessons with his readers and listeners.

His publications thus far are of the personal/professional self-help, self-improvement genre and systematically offer valuable sage advice on specific topics.

His writing style can be described as being conversational. As an author Rae strives to have a one-to-one conversation with each of his readers, very much like having your own personal self-development coach.

Rae is known for having a wry sense of humor that features in his publications. To learn more about Rae A. Stonehouse, **visit The Wonderful World of Rae Stonehouse** at https://raestonehouse.com

Facebook: https://www.facebook.com/raestonehouse.aws

Twitter: https://twitter.com/raestonehouse

ALSO BY RAE A. STONEHOUSE

Power of Promotion: On-line Marketing for Toastmasters Club Growth

https://books2read.com/powerofpromotion

You're Hired! Job Search Strategies That Work (This is the complete program)

E-book & Paperback: https://yourehirednow.com

On-line E-course: (Available as a self-directed or instructor-led program) https://liveforexcellenceacademy.com/

You're Hired! Resume Tactics: Job Search Strategies That Work

E-book & Paperback: https://resumetactics.online

On-line E-course: https://liveforexcellenceacademy.com/

Job Interview Preparation: Job Search Strategies That Work

E-book & Paperback: https://jobinterviewpreparation.online/

On-line E-course: https://liveforexcellenceacademy.com/

You're Hired! Leveraging Your Network: Job Search Strategies That Work

E-book & Paperback: https://leveragingyournetwork.online/

On-line E-course: https://liveforexcellenceacademy.com/

~~~

You're Hired! Power Tactics: Job Search Strategies That Work

(This is an e-box set containing the complete content of Resume Tactics, Job Interview Preparation & Leveraging Your Network)

E-book: https://powertactics.online/

~~~

Power Networking for Shy People: How to Network Like a Pro

E-book & **Paperback:** https://powernetworkingforshypeople.ca

~~~

The Savvy Emcee: How to be a Dynamic Master of Ceremonies

E-book: https://thesavvyemcee.com

~~~

Working With Words: How to Add Life to Your Oral Presentations

E-book & **Paperback:** https://workingwithwordsbook.com/

Also available as an on-line course at https://liveforexcellenceacademy.com

~~~

Blow Your Own Horn! Personal Branding for Business Professionals

E-book & **Paperback:** https://blowyourownhorn.online/

~~~

Make It Safe! A Family Caregiver's Home Safety Assessment Guide For Supporting Elders@Home https://makeitsafe.online.

Make It Safe! A Family Caregiver's Home Safety Assessment Guide For Supporting Elders@Home – Companion Workbook
https://makeitsafe.online.

Also available as an on-line course at https://liveforexcellenceacademy.com

If you have found this book and program to be helpful, please leave us a warm review wherever you purchased this book.

www.ingramcontent.com/pod-product-compliance
Lightning Source LLC
Chambersburg PA
CBHW070910030426
42336CB00014BA/2361